FRESS

This book is dedicated to my girls—Madeline, Eleanor, Hannah, and Sophie. May you never have to scrabble around trying to piece together ragged old bits of paper with vague instructions on them to cook my food.

An Hachette UK Company
www.hachette.co.uk

First published in Great Britain in 2017 by Mitchell Beazley,
a division of Octopus Publishing Group Ltd., Carmelite House,
50 Victoria Embankment, London EC4Y 0DZ
www.octopusbooks.co.uk

Design and layout copyright © Octopus Publishing Group 2017
Text copyright © Emma Spitzer 2017
Photography copyright © Clare Winfield 2017

Distributed in the US by Hachette Book Group,
1290 Avenue of the Americas, 4th and 5th Floors,
New York, NY 10020

Distributed in Canada by Canadian Manda Group,
664 Annette St., Toronto, Ontario, Canada M6S 2C8

ISBN 978-1-78472-298-2

Printed and bound in China.

10 9 8 7 6 5 4 3 2 1

Publisher's Note
This book contains dishes made with raw or lightly cooked eggs. Once prepared these dishes should be kept refrigerated and used promptly. The USDA advises that eggs should not be consumed raw, and does not recommend eating raw shell eggs that are not cooked or are undercooked due to the possibility that Salmonella bacteria may be present. Infants and young children, pregnant women, older adults, and people with weakened immune systems caused by cancer treatment, diabetes, AIDS, and bone marrow and organ transplants are at greatest risk for foodborne illness and should avoid uncooked or lightly cooked dishes made with eggs.

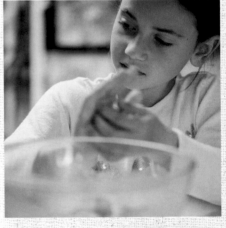

Publisher: Alison Starling
Senior Editor: Leanne Bryan
Copy Editor: Jo Richardson
Art Director: Juliette Norsworthy
Designers: Naomi Edmondson and Ella McLean
Photographer: Clare Winfield
Food Stylist: Rosie Reynolds
Props Stylist: Linda Berlin
Illustrator: Ella McLean
Americanizer: Constance Novis
Senior Production Manager: Katherine Hockley

FRESS

Def. *(verb)* "to eat copiously
and without restraint"

Bold flavors from
a Jewish kitchen

EMMA
SPITZER

Contents

Introduction

I have been cooking since I was eight years old, and never having concentrated much at school, food was the only thing that really held my attention. My mother was not a passionate cook, so I can't claim that my love of cooking was inherited, but she was a good cook and always made sure we had a homemade dinner on the table every night. Most of these dishes were part of the legacy of hearty and homely recipes like stuffed cabbage leaves and pot roast from my Polish grandmother, whom I sadly never met, passed down to her in the customary way of every Jewish mother when her daughter gets married. My mother also drew inspiration from the doyennes of Jewish cuisine of her time, such as Evelyn Rose and Florence Greenberg, the results of which included her legendary fried fish balls and rum chocolate mousse.

My cultural heritage is something of a melting pot, with my paternal grandparents coming from Russia in addition to my maternal grandparents hailing from the ghettos of Warsaw, although my parents were both born in the UK. My sisters and I traveled a lot through the Middle East and the Mediterranean as kids and the greatest lasting impression of those cultural expeditions was always the food. I remember sitting in a gas station at the border between Israel and Lebanon eating warm pitta bread with the best hummus I have ever tasted. It was how people ate out in that part of the country; little kitchens everywhere, from dusty roadside stands to tiny restaurants in the middle of nowhere, serving dishes that left strong imprints on my memory.

The happiest times in my life have always been associated with the three things I cherish the most: family, food, and travel. My family wasn't religious and didn't keep kosher, but we had a strong Jewish identity and food played the biggest part in shaping this. Friday night was the one night of the week that was sacred and the only night we would all eat together as a family. I would come home from school to the waft of roast chicken, the windows all steamy from the pot of golden chicken soup simmering away on the stove. What made the soup that much more special were the particular extras that went into it—the little yellow croutons, the *lokshen* (egg noodles), and tiny golden eggs. Mom would always tell us to watch out for the peppercorns, and as I strain these out of the soup now for my own kids, I wonder why she didn't do the same to spare us the mini incendiary explosions of spice. Then came the fight after the meal to see who could get to the roasting pan first to scrape off all the burnt-on onions, chicken bits, and roast potato bottoms.

Food and travel were very much interlinked for me. Establishing a successful career in publishing and advertising in my early twenties wasn't enough to satisfy my aspirations and I fantasized about eating my way around various continents and landscapes. Having been fortunate enough to travel widely as a child, I felt there was more to discover, so I took a year off and embarked on a solo voyage around the world. On return, my eyes wider and my wallet smaller, I paid a visit to Leiths School of Food and Wine to see if I could train as a chef. I had eaten so much amazing and interesting food on my travels, I just wanted to be able to cook as well as I ate. But the diploma course proved too expensive for me, since I had used up all my savings. My ambition was put on hold while I went back to my former career in publishing, although this time I was working for a travel publisher, so it was almost my dream job, as I was paid to travel and stay in some of the world's finest hotels. I ate like a queen.

When I set up my own travel business in 2002, I barely had time to cook and relied on the vibrant food scene in Camden, in north London, where I lived and worked. Getting married and having children re-ignited my desire to cook. I am by nature a very ambitious and determined person, so the more I cooked, the better I wanted to be. I secretly always felt that I had a lot to live up to, having a fantastic cook for a mother-in-law; a girl's worst nightmare. My mother-in-law Judith's mother was born in Algeria, in North Africa, before emigrating to Jerusalem, in Israel, where she raised Judith along with her eight siblings. Safta, as she was known, which translates as "grandmother," was a tremendous cook and would regularly host banquets for all the family and their friends. There is much talk around the table to this day of these legendary Moroccan feasts, attended by more people than available table space and chairs. A big couscousière would contain a pot of meat, vegetables, and fresh herbs at the bottom, with grains of semolina in the top slowly being steamed in the aromatic vapors from the soup below to make the couscous. There were also spicy fish stews accompanied by side dishes of *mahkuda*, a Moroccan-style tortilla, and *matbucha*, a hot salad of paprika-smothered bell peppers and tomatoes. They say that Safta stopped living when she had to stop cooking, such was the imperative nature of her gift of effortless hospitality. But the memories of her food live on through Judith as she fondly continues to cook and serve some of her greatest food legacies, and I am extremely proud to be the custodian, in turn, of some of those much-loved and cherished recipes.

I call them recipes in the loosest sense, as they had no formulaic measures or clear written methods, just the notes my mother-in-law made in her head and those I've since written down in a bid to preserve these sacred North African delicacies. Judith deeply regrets not having asked her mother to keep those recipes in a journal, so I hope this book helps to lessen some of that regret when she sees the dishes she worked so hard to recreate in black and white.

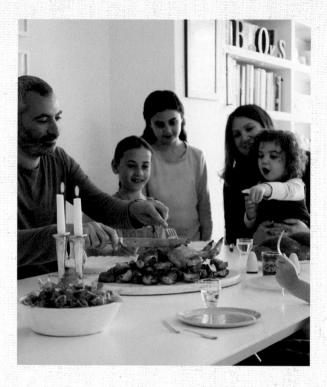

In a similar vein, my own recipes for this book have been far harder to write than they have been to cook because I only ever quantify ingredients precisely when I'm baking, so it has been hard to narrow down my normal sausage-finger pinches into teaspoons and contain my freestyle herb-throwing into handfuls. I can only encourage you to be as open-minded in your judgment of what you think will work best for your palate and regard my recipes (baking and anything else technical aside) as approximate guidelines. So feel free to be less heavy-handed with any fiery spices, as I could quite happily scatter raw chiles on almost anything savory and devour them without hesitation, but appreciate that other people may have a more sensitive reaction to spice.

For the last decade or so, my life has been chaotic to say the least; with four young kids and working full time in the travel business I founded with my sister, you could say that my plate was already pretty full. Entering *MasterChef* took that chaos to a whole new level. I call it my "life begins" moment, the point at which I was ready to see whether my passion for cooking was just that or if there was more to discover. I had been a huge fan of the show for many years and always dreamed of sitting at a table with John Torode and Gregg Wallace eating my food. I had no idea that that dream would become a reality or how much it would change my life.

In *MasterChef*, you are asked continually to push the boundaries and the pressure is on every time you cook to produce better results than at the previous stage, so it becomes a grueling process of experimentation. I lived in my kitchen day and night, trying out different combinations of ingredients and seasonings that drew on both my husband's and my rich cultural heritage, and my passion for the flavors of the Levant and North Africa. I relished the fact that I was producing dishes that neither John nor Gregg had ever eaten before. You would have thought after all their years of judging that there couldn't be many more surprises in store for them, but having dug deep into my unique culinary treasure trove and translated those precious passed-down dishes into the contemporary culinary language, I wowed them with my unusual flavor combinations.

During this period of intensive activity, if my girls wanted to spend time with me, they had to get involved with me in the kitchen—it was a case

of pure selfishness on my part. They ate almost everything I cooked. Being a part of the process meant that they learned so much about food and different flavors, and at the same time it taught me that kids eat much better when they see their meal as a sort of accomplishment. Consequently, I never adapt my dishes for younger palates; as far as I'm concerned, kids' food just means a smaller portion and not something different altogether. My recipes are designed to be enjoyed by the whole family, hands big and small digging into sharing plates in the middle of the table. When kids get to help themselves to food, it's amazing what they end up putting on their plates and eating. And using spices doesn't necessarily result in spicy food, just nice warm flavors that sit in the background; if you want spice heat, it can easily be added separately to spare the kids who might dislike it.

My only objective when I started *MasterChef* was not to be disqualified in the first round, being well aware that I didn't fit the typical *MasterChef* mold. My style of food erred on the generous side, with dishes made to share and rip into at the table— rustic rather than elegant fine dining. I therefore had the added constant task of striving to present my food in a more esthetically appealing way, mindful that the program viewers could only see my food, not taste it. So that forced me to think about my cooking in a different way, for which I will forever be thankful.

Reaching the finals of *MasterChef* was beyond my wildest expectations. I managed to impress some of the harshest critics—William Sitwell and Charles Campion to name but two—and this gave me the confidence to really believe in myself. Having learned so much during the competition, this was the most important lesson—that confidence is king in the kitchen and a little self-belief can go a long way. John Torode once declared that confident cooks produce confident food, and he wasn't wrong there.

My newfound confidence has resulted in this book where I share with you my favorite recipes from a heritage of which I am fiercely proud, and that I believe every home cook can easily recreate in their own kitchen. Here in London, for example, we've been so fortunate to have experienced a revival of many Jewish and Middle Eastern classics through the likes of Yotam Ottolenghi and Honey & Co. I am sure this is true elsewhere, too, so this book is not having to break new ground and introduce people to an unfamiliar cuisine. It offers instead an approachable way to prepare these dishes from one home cook to another, my principal aim being to inspire confidence in others in the kitchen and encourage a greater use of spices to enhance everyday humble ingredients. Above all, I see my food as comfort food—in a good way. It is uncomplicated and (mostly) unfussy, as well as enjoyable to cook!

My family tree

Grandpa Samuel (Polish)

Grandma Celia (Austrian)

Bubba Rose (Polish)

Grandpa Egon (Czech)

Grandpa Harry (Russian)

Safta (Algerian)

Hilary Barnett (British)

Simon Spitzer (British)

Sabba (Algerian)

Grandma Myra (Spanish)

Bernard Barnett (British)

Judith Spitzer (Israeli)

Emma

Carl

Deborah (Emma's sister)

Samantha (Emma's sister)

Natalie (Carl's sister)

Nicole (Carl's sister)

Eleanor

Madeline

Hannah

Sophie

Kitchen-cupboard ingredients

Almost all the ingredients you need for making the recipes in this book are widely available from major supermarkets, specialist grocery stores, or food websites.

The following are some of the most useful food items you will need:

Eggs These are always large unless otherwise specified, and I always use organic free-range.

Fresh herbs Since quantities vary depending on where and how you buy them, it's hard to give specific measurements for herbs; a supermarket package can be around 1 ounce, while bunches of herbs from Middle Eastern and Asian grocers or supermarkets weigh in at around 5 ounces. I have therefore generally indicated measures of herbs in handfuls, but you can always use your own judgment. Start with less and add more if you are unsure.

Oils I mostly use canola or corn oil for frying, as it has a higher smoking point. I use olive oil for gentle frying, and a good-quality extra virgin olive oil is essential for dressings and drizzling. However, never use extra virgin for frying because it creates harmful free radicals if heated to a high temperature.

Salt and pepper The king and queen of seasonings. Unless otherwise specified, I use sea salt for a more subtle flavor on dishes such as salads and dips, and as a garnish before serving. Black pepper is always freshly ground from peppercorns and not the pre-packaged ready-ground stuff.

Stocks and stock powders I'm a real heathen when it comes to stock, as I love the powdered variety. Fresh stock has its place and I always made my own when the kids were babies, as I was terrified of the high salt content in ready-made stocks. Now I simply adjust the amount of additional salt when using powdered stock such as chicken flavor soup and seasoning mix (I like Osem or Thelma) from the kosher section of the supermarket, which I use in every recipe that calls for chicken stock.

Spices

I'm somewhat of a spice junkie—it was a running joke in the *MasterChef* studio that everyone knew which bench was mine from the number of spices on it. My passion stems from visits to exotic markets with my family from a young age and the hours spent walking around taking in all the foreign smells. I have my favorite spices that I just can't manage without, namely cumin, coriander, and sumac, but I also love the heady scents of paprika and the earthy tang of za'atar. In fact, I have at least 30 jars of colorful and fragrant concoctions from all over the world stored in my most organized drawer in the house.

Spices can add a real depth of complexity and turn ordinary, everyday dishes into something quite extraordinary and, because many of the recipes throughout the book call for the same spices, I can assure you that your purchases will not end up in what I call the "spice graveyard" at the back of a cupboard. I would recommend that you invest in some small jars, label them, and make them as accessible as possible so that you don't have to remove the entire contents of your cupboard to find them each time. I have also included alternative spices where there are comparable substitutes in the recipes.

I would always recommend toasting and grinding whole spices in bulk so that you have a constant supply on hand; the flavor is infinitely better and the spices will keep fresh for months sealed in an airtight jar. The best equipment for grinding spices is either a power blender, a coffee grinder, or a hand-held stick blender. A mortar and pestle will work well too, and build some good arm muscle in the process; just sift the spices afterward to remove any coarse bits.

My top 10 spices

Aleppo pepper (*see* page 44)

baharat (a Middle Eastern spice mixture that includes cumin, coriander, cinnamon, paprika, nutmeg, cloves, cardamom, and black pepper)

caraway seeds

coriander

cumin

Lebanese 7-spice Mix (*see* page 14)

ras el hanout (a North African mixture of many different spices including cardamom, clove, nutmeg, allspice, fennel, cinnamon, coriander, cumin, paprika, black pepper, and sometimes dried rosebuds)

smoked paprika

sumac

Za'atar (*see* page 15)

A note on equipment

Since my food is designed to be relatively uncomplicated and easy to cook, no fancy artillery is required other than some simple tools to make the process more pleasurable, and you are likely to have most of the kitchen equipment needed to prepare the recipes. However, when a specific type of equipment is required this is mentioned in the recipes.

This lovely warm spice mixture, heavy with black pepper and cinnamon, is the perfect partner for all manner of dishes, especially my Chicken Shawarma with Jerusalem and Lebanese Spices (*see* page 76) and Sephardi Rice with Vermicelli and Lentils (*see* page 155). I therefore recommend that you keep a batch permanently on hand.

Lebanese 7-spice Mix

Makes about ½ cup

2 tablespoons freshly ground black pepper
2 tablespoons ground allspice
2 tablespoons ground cinnamon
2 teaspoons freshly grated nutmeg
2 teaspoons ground cumin
1 teaspoon ground cloves
1 teaspoon ground ginger

Put all the spices into a bowl and mix together.

Transfer to an airtight container, seal securely, and store in a cool, dark place for up to 6 months.

Tip

If you have a spice grinder or power blender, substitute whole spices for the ready-ground spices. Toast in a dry skillet over medium heat until they start to smell fragrant, shaking the pan constantly, then blitz to a coarse powder.

Za'atar is more commonly used throughout the Middle East and the Mediterranean as a table condiment than a spice. It's just as good mixed into a paste with some olive oil for dipping bread into as it is as a crust for meat or fish, or sprinkled over salads. I learned how to make my own version in Jordan and wanted to share this simple recipe so that your kitchen cupboard need never be without it.

Za'atar

Makes about 1 cup

¼ cup sesame seeds
½ cup dried thyme (not wild)
1 teaspoon olive oil
2 tablespoons ground sumac
2 tablespoons chickpea flour
¼ teaspoon table salt

Heat a dry skillet over medium heat, add the sesame seeds, and toast until they are golden brown and starting to smell nutty, shaking the pan constantly. Transfer to a bowl and set aside.

Add the thyme to a spice grinder or power blender and blitz until powdery in texture. Spread out on a plate. Add the olive oil to the palm of your hand and rub your hands together, then gradually work it into the thyme, just coating it with the oil on your hands.

Stir the thyme into the sesame seeds with the sumac, chickpea flour, and salt, making sure that everything is mixed together well.

Transfer to an airtight container, seal securely, and store in a cool, dark place for up to 3 months.

Dukkah translates from the Arabic as "to pound" and its origin lies in Egypt, where a combination of nuts, herbs, and spices are broken down together into a paste or powder and served as a dip with bread, or used as a crust for meat, fish, or vegetables. I created my own concoction for my "calling card" dish on *MasterChef* to make a crust for my rack of lamb. I use this on all manner of dishes, but always serve a bowl of it with some top-quality olive oil with bread as a pre-dinner nibble.

Dukkah

Makes 4 servings

2 tablespoons sesame seeds
½ cup unsalted pistachio nuts
2 tablespoons ground cumin
2 tablespoons ground coriander
2 teaspoons ground sumac
sea salt
small handful of flat-leaf parsley leaves, coarsely chopped

Heat a dry skillet over medium heat, add the sesame seeds and pistachio nuts, and toast for around 5 minutes until lightly golden and fragrant, shaking the pan constantly.

Transfer to a food processor along with the cumin, coriander, sumac, salt to taste, and the parsley and pulse until the nuts are finely chopped but still have some texture.

It will keep really well for up to a month if sealed in an airtight container and stored in the fridge.

This powerful Tunisian chile paste is one of the greatest condiments you can have in your fridge. I have experimented with many variations, but this recipe is the one I am happiest with. The sun-dried tomatoes are not a traditional addition to harissa, but I love the flavor they bring as a foil for the strong heat of the chile. Serve with some olive oil drizzled over the top as a dip for crusty bread, or mix into yogurt, mayonnaise, or ketchup to spice them up for use as condiments. Harissa adds a serious depth of flavor to sauces and works really well in marinades, too.

Harissa

Makes about 8 ounces

10 dried red chiles
2 red bell peppers
1 tablespoon cumin seeds
1 tablespoon coriander seeds
1 teaspoon caraway seeds
2 garlic cloves, peeled and halved
1 teaspoon smoked paprika
1 teaspoon sea salt
2 long red chiles, seeded and coarsely chopped
3 sun-dried tomatoes in oil, drained
1 tablespoon red wine vinegar
½ cup canola oil

Soak the dried chiles in hot water for 30 minutes. Drain, then trim off the stalks. Seed and coarsely chop the chiles (it is advisable to wear gloves for this prep, to protect yourself from the burning effects of the chiles).

Preheat the broiler to high. Place the bell peppers under the broiler for around 10 to 15 minutes, turning once, until the skins have blackened. Transfer to a resealable plastic food bag and seal, or to a bowl and immediately cover with plastic wrap, then let stand for about 20 minutes until cool enough to handle and the skins have loosened. Remove the skins with the back of a knife and discard the stalks and seeds, then coarsely chop the flesh.

Heat a dry skillet over medium heat, add the cumin, coriander, and caraway seeds and toast for 3 minutes, shaking the pan constantly to ensure that they don't burn. Transfer to a mortar and pestle or spice grinder or powder blender (*see* page 13) and grind to a coarse powder.

Place the garlic cloves along with the ground spices, paprika, and salt in a food processor and pulse until finely chopped. Add the fresh chiles, dried chiles, and sun-dried tomatoes and pulse a few times to combine. Lastly, add the vinegar and oil and blend until you have a coarse paste.

Add to an 8-ounce sterilized preserving jar (*see* page 144), seal securely, and store in the fridge for up to a month.

Small plates for sharing

One of the first High Holidays I spent with my in-laws was Rosh Hashanah, or Jewish New Year. I can clearly remember an extraordinary feast that spread the entire length of two big tables, but it was the bright red bowls of matbucha that really caught my attention. This is the dish that is most often requested by the family because it's pure nostalgia for them, having been made by my husband's grandmother Safta throughout their lives. The head of the family, Safta bore nine children and for many years raised them all by herself. Her legendary cooking is the subject of many family dinners. I can't say whether my matbucha matches up to Safta's, but I can say that it's delicious and the dish that I am most frequently asked to contribute to the table. Matbucha can be eaten with all manner of accompaniments, such as Labneh (*see* page 47), flatbreads, and olives; it's worth making a huge batch and freezing the excess—there is no such thing as too much when it comes to this dish.

Matbucha

Serves 12 as part of a meze spread

6 large red bell peppers, halved, cores and seeds removed

3 tablespoons olive oil, plus extra for drizzling over the bell peppers

6 very ripe large (but not beefsteak) tomatoes

3 large garlic cloves, minced

2 large red chiles, seeded if you want less heat, and finely chopped

2 tablespoons sweet paprika

2 teaspoons sea salt

freshly ground black pepper

1 to 2 pinches of sugar, to taste

Preheat the broiler to its highest setting and line a baking pan with foil. Place the bell peppers, cut-side down, on the pan. Drizzle with olive oil, rubbing the oil over the skins to ensure they are well covered. Place under the broiler for around 15 to 20 minutes until they are nicely charred on top. Remove from the pan, transfer to a plastic food bag or a bowl, and seal the bag or cover the bowl with plastic wrap. Let stand for 20 minutes or until the skins have loosened and the bell peppers are cool enough to handle.

Meanwhile, score the bottoms of the tomatoes in a crisscross shape and add to a large bowl. Cover with boiling water and let stand for 1 minute. Drain the tomatoes and peel off the skins. Cut the tomatoes in half and scoop the insides out into a bowl for using later. Chop the tomatoes into medium-sized dice and set aside.

Once the bell peppers are cool, peel off the skins. Chop the flesh into strips.

Heat the measured olive oil in a large, heavy saucepan, add the garlic and chiles, and gently fry for a couple of minutes, being careful not to burn them. Add the peppers and tomatoes, sprinkle them with the paprika, then season with the salt and black pepper to taste. Give the mixture a good stir, turn the heat down to a simmer, and cook gently for around 2 to 3 hours, stirring every so often. If you need a little more liquid, add the reserved tomato insides to a sieve and let them drain into the pan. If the mixture is reducing too quickly, cover the pan with a lid and continue to simmer over low heat.

Once the matbucha is the desired consistency, add the sugar to taste and check for seasoning. Remove from the heat and let cool. The matbucha can be served hot or cold. It can be stored, sealed in an airtight container, in the fridge for up to 5 days, or frozen for future use.

On one of my periodical health kicks (usually in January), I decided to make this dip in the way it was intended, that is with plain yogurt and minimal oil, which means it's tasty but virtuous. However, when you add a little more olive oil and some crème fraîche, it's transformed into a really creamy, delicious, and indulgent treat. This works very well as a dip or a lovely addition to a meze spread, accompanied by Hummus (*see* page 25) and Challah (*see* page 204). The Israelis make something similar using mayonnaise, so I still consider this to be a marginally healthier option.

Creamy Eggplant Dip

Serves 6

4 good-sized eggplants

table salt, for sprinkling

3 tablespoons olive oil, divided

2 large onions, minced

3 garlic cloves, crushed

2 tablespoons crème fraîche
(or Greek yogurt)

sea salt and freshly ground black pepper

Trim the eggplants, then slice them into ½-inch thick disks. Sprinkle both sides with table salt. Let stand for 10 minutes in a colander in the sink to allow some of the bitter juices to drain.

Preheat the broiler to medium-high. Rinse the salt from the eggplant slices and pat dry, then brush each side with a tablespoon of the olive oil and season with sea salt and black pepper.

Cook under the broiler for around 7 minutes on each side, then remove from the broiler and let stand until they are cool enough to handle.

Meanwhile, heat the remaining olive oil in a skillet, add the onions, and fry gently for around 10 to 15 minutes until they are soft and slightly caramelized. Add the garlic and cook for a further 5 minutes.

Remove the skins from the eggplant and finely chop the flesh with a knife—you don't need to be precise here, as it's nice to retain some texture. Add to a bowl with the onions and garlic and crème fraîche (or yogurt) and season to taste with sea salt and black pepper.

This is lovely served at room temperature. It will keep well for up to 4 days, sealed in an airtight container, in the fridge.

This creamy chickpea dip needs little introduction, so famous is it in its own right, and there are numerous restaurants and street-food outlets as well as large sections of Middle Eastern supermarkets dedicated to showcasing its many different varieties. I may be biased, but I think my father-in-law, a.k.a. Bugga, makes the best version of all, and we are lucky enough to enjoy it at almost every family gathering with some warm pitta bread, Challah (*see* page 204), or my personal favorite, some salted potato chips. View the recipe as a blank canvas and feel free to add any kind of topping you fancy to make it even more special; it's all about personal taste, so don't take these quantities too literally.

Hummus

Serves 6 to 8

2 × 14oz cans chickpeas, drained and liquid reserved

juice of 1 to 2 lemons

2 garlic cloves, crushed, or to taste

1 tablespoon tahini, or to taste

1 teaspoon soy sauce, or to taste

3 tablespoons olive oil, plus a little extra for garnish

1 teaspoon sea salt, or to taste

pinch of ground sumac, to garnish (optional)

Put the chickpeas, reserving 1 tablespoon for garnish, the juice of 1 lemon, the garlic, tahini, and soy sauce in a food processor and blend for a few seconds until you have a thick paste.

With the motor running, gradually add the oil and 2 tablespoons of the reserved chickpea liquid. At this point it would be wise to taste the hummus before adding the remaining lemon juice and the salt. Blend for a couple of minutes until you have the right consistency, adding any of the above ingredients as you see fit.

Transfer the mixture to a serving bowl and drizzle it with some extra olive oil. Garnish with a pinch of sumac, if you like, and the reserved chickpeas.

It can be stored for up to 5 days, sealed in an airtight container, in the fridge.

Topping suggestions

* Cut 2 pieces of pitta bread into small squares and shallow-fry in vegetable oil in a skillet until golden brown. Remove and drain on paper towels, then place on top of the hummus with a little extra olive oil and some chopped flat-leaf parsley.

* Lightly toast a handful of pine nuts in 1 tablespoon of vegetable oil in a skillet until golden brown. Scatter them onto the hummus and then sprinkle with a generous pinch of sweet paprika.

I was fortunate enough to inherit this recipe from a friend of mine, Julian. Over dinner one night, he spoke at length about life growing up on a kibbutz in Israel and how big family banquets using the locally grown ingredients were the mainstay of his childhood. While he discussed all the different dishes his father used to make with great passion, it was this eggplant recipe that clearly ignited the most fire in this voice.

The great thing about this dish is its versatility. It will sit amazingly well on a cold buffet spread, as well as served hot on top of couscous or rice with a dollop of crème fraîche and a nice green salad for a great vegetarian pleaser. Either way, it seems to improve with age, so I would encourage you to make it ahead and let it stand for a couple of days in the fridge before using.

Fried Eggplant in Tomato Sauce

Serves 6 as part of a meze spread or 4 as a main

2 large eggplants
⅓ cup olive oil, divided
2 teaspoons sea salt, or to taste
1 large onion, thinly sliced
2 × 14oz cans really good-quality diced tomatoes
2 tablespoons tomato paste
3 tablespoons water
1 tablespoon superfine sugar, or to taste
1 tablespoon red wine vinegar
½ teaspoon ground cumin
toasted flatbread, to serve (optional)

Trim the eggplants, then slice them into ½-inch thick disks. Heat 2 tablespoons of the oil in a large skillet over medium-high heat. Add enough of the eggplant slices to make a single layer, sprinkle with some of the salt, and fry gently for around 5 to 8 minutes or until they are golden brown on both sides. Transfer to a plate lined with paper towels. Repeat with the remaining eggplant slices, adding a little more of the oil to the pan as needed, and then let cool.

While the eggplants are cooling, add the remaining oil to the same skillet and fry the onion with a pinch of salt over medium heat until translucent; this will take approximately 10 minutes.

Add the canned tomatoes, tomato paste, measured water, and sugar to the skillet and give the mixture a good stir. Cook over low heat until the mixture has reduced to a thick consistency, stirring every so often; this will take around 30 minutes, but stay close to the skillet so that you can keep an eye on it.

Cut the cooled eggplant slices in half and gently incorporate them into the sauce. Cover the skillet with a lid and let simmer gently for 10 minutes. Add the vinegar and cumin and mix well, gently breaking down the eggplants to form a thick but not smooth consistency. Taste for seasoning, adding a pinch more salt or sugar if needed.

Remove the skillet from the heat and either serve immediately or, even better, let cool and serve at room temperature accompanied by toasted flatbread, if liked.

I have a real love and fascination for these little Polish pillows. When my maternal grandparents came to the UK from the ghettos of Warsaw in the 1930s, just like many other immigrants, as Anglophiles they assimilated as best they could into their new life. Where they did stick firmly to their Polish ways, however, was in cooking. My grandmother died before I was born, so I never had the opportunity to try her pierogi firsthand and have just had to settle for secondhand instruction. But I have stayed true to her style by making a classic mixture of potato and onion, with a few little twists of my own.

Caramelized Onion and Potato Pierogi

Makes around 40 to 45 pierogi

For the pierogi dough
2½ cups all-purpose flour, plus extra for kneading, if needed, and dusting
½ teaspoon salt
3 tablespoons unsalted butter, cubed
1 large egg, lightly beaten
¼ cup sour cream

For the filling
3 tablespoons vegetable oil
2 large white onions, finely diced
1¾ cups cubed, peeled white potatoes
½ teaspoon sea salt, or to taste
¼ teaspoon ground white pepper, or to taste
3 tablespoons fresh cheese

To serve
½ cup sour cream
1 tablespoon fresh lemon juice

Start by making the dough. If you have a food processor, add all the ingredients to it and pulse until the mixture comes together into a sticky dough. If making by hand, add the flour and salt to a bowl. Using your fingertips, gently work the butter into the flour until the mixture resembles bread crumbs, then mix in the egg and sour cream to make a dough.

Knead the dough using your fingertips on a floured work surface for 5 minutes, adding a little more flour if it is too sticky. Seal in plastic wrap and let rest in the fridge for a minimum of 30 minutes while you prepare the filling.

Heat the oil in a large skillet, add the onions, and gently fry over very low heat for around 30 minutes until golden brown, stirring often. Drain the onions in a sieve, reserving the oil.

Cook the potatoes in a saucepan of boiling water for 20 minutes, then drain and mash. Mix the mashed potatoes and onions together and season with the salt and white pepper. Let the mixture cool, then add the fresh cheese and mix in thoroughly. Check the seasoning.

Roll out the dough on a heavily floured work surface until 1/16 inch thick. Using a 3½-inch round cookie cutter, cut out circles from the dough, rerolling the trimmings to make more circles.

Place a heaped teaspoonful of the filling in the center of each circle. Fold over to make a semicircle, then dampen your fingers with water and seal the edges.

Bring a large saucepan of salted water to a boil, drop in the pierogi, in batches, and boil for 5 minutes. Remove with a slotted spoon and drain.

Meanwhile, mix the sour cream and lemon juice together in a bowl ready for serving.

Heat 1 tablespoon of the reserved oil in a large skillet and fry the pierogi, in batches, for 1 to 2 minutes on each side until golden brown.

Serve the crispy pierogi hot with the sour cream mixture for dipping.

I spent a long time experimenting with alternative Ashkenazi-style flavors in order to create a unique and tasty pierogi that my grandmother would have been proud of. The combination of salt beef, mustard, and dill is a classic one, and works really well when dipped into the accompanying dill and mustard sauce.

Pastrami and Sauerkraut Pierogi with Dill and Mustard Sauce

Makes around 40 to 45 pierogi

1 quantity Pierogi Dough (*see* opposite)
all-purpose flour, for dusting
vegetable oil, for shallow-frying
salt

For the filling
1 cup cooled mashed potatoes
2¼oz pastrami, chopped into small pieces
3 tablespoons drained sauerkraut
½ cucumber pickle spear, finely chopped
1 teaspoon prepared English mustard
½ teaspoon celery salt
pinch of sea salt, or to taste

For the dill and mustard sauce
3 tablespoons Dijon mustard
1 tablespoon white wine vinegar
½ cup canola oil
2 tablespoons finely chopped dill
½ teaspoon sea salt
pinch of ground white pepper (optional)

Mix all the ingredients for the filling together in a large bowl and check for seasoning.

Roll out the pierogi dough on a heavily floured work surface until ¹⁄₁₆ inch thick. Using a 3½-inch round cookie cutter, cut out circles from the dough, rerolling the trimmings to make more circles.

Place a heaped teaspoonful of the filling in the center of each circle. Fold over to make a semicircle, then dampen your fingers with water and seal the edges.

Bring a large saucepan of salted water to a boil, drop in the peirogi, in batches, and boil for 5 minutes. Remove with a slotted spoon and drain on a dish cloth.

Meanwhile, to make the sauce, mix the mustard and vinegar together in a bowl. Add the oil in a very slow trickle, whisking constantly, until it has all been incorporated, then stir in the remaining ingredients.

Heat 1 tablespoon of oil in a large skillet and fry the pierogi, in batches, for 1 to 2 minutes on each side until golden brown.

Serve the crispy pierogi hot with the sauce on the side for dipping.

Tips

* You can omit the last step of frying and just enjoy the pierogi boiled.

* The pierogi freeze beautifully—just place them on a cookie sheet in a single layer and open freeze them before sealing them in a resealable plastic freezer bag.

I first had *kibbeh* in Tel Aviv, Israel, in the Carmel Market, one of the largest food markets in the country, and the second time in a fantastic restaurant called Shoshanna. There are as many variations of this wonderful Middle Eastern dish as there are spellings of it. This is the street-food version; deep-fried and crispy with a lovely warm lamb filling. I view it as a form of cooking therapy when I make these, allowing enough time to try and get the shells really thin and the shape as authentically like a torpedo as possible.

Lamb Kibbeh with Green Tahini

Makes around 20 kibbeh

2 cups coarse bulgur wheat
1 white onion, coarsely chopped
1lb 2oz ground lamb
1 teaspoon salt
freshly ground black pepper
vegetable oil, for deep-frying
lemon wedges, to serve

For the filling
2 tablespoons olive oil, divided
1 white onion, minced
3 garlic cloves, minced
2 tablespoons pine nuts
1lb 2oz ground lamb
1 teaspoon Lebanese 7-spice Mix
(see page 14)
1 teaspoon ground cumin
1 teaspoon ground coriander
1 teaspoon ground sumac
½ teaspoon ground cinnamon
handful of chopped flat-leaf parsley
1 teaspoon sea salt, or to taste
freshly ground black pepper, or to taste

For the green tahini
2 tablespoons tahini
1 garlic clove, crushed
juice of ½ lemon
pinch of sea salt
large handful of finely chopped flat-leaf
parsley or cilantro
freshly ground black pepper

Soak the bulgur in plenty of cold water for at least 30 minutes. Drain and squeeze out the excess water in a clean dish cloth or cheesecloth. Add to a bowl with the onion, lamb, salt, and some pepper, and mix together well. Then transfer small amounts of the mixture to your food processor and process until you have smooth, doughlike consistency. Cover and let chill in the fridge while you make the filling.

Heat 1 tablespoon of the oil in a skillet, add the onion, and cook gently for around 10 minutes until soft and translucent. Add the garlic and pine nuts and cook for a couple more minutes before adding the lamb, breaking it up with a wooden spoon. Mix all the spices together in a small bowl, then combine with the remaining tablespoon of oil to make a paste. Stir the paste into the meat mixture along with the parsley, add the salt and some pepper, and fry until the lamb has just cooked through. At this point, check the seasoning and adjust if necessary. Let the filling cool for 15 minutes.

To assemble the kibbeh, take a golf ball-sized amount of the bulgur and meat mixture, roll into a ball, and press your middle finger into the center to make a hole for the filling, turning the ball around a few times on your finger to make the hole deep enough. Place 1 to 2 teaspoonfuls of the filling in the hole and pinch the top of the ball to seal (wet your hands if the mixture gets too sticky), then reshape into a ball or form into the more traditional torpedo shape. Preheat the oven to 225°F.

Heat the oil for deep-frying in a deep-fat fryer or a large saucepan (don't fill the pan more than halfway) to around 340°F. Deep-fry the kibbeh, in batches, for around 10 minutes until golden. Remove with a slotted spoon and drain on a plate lined with paper towels, then keep the cooked kibbeh warm in the oven while you fry the rest.

Meanwhile, for the green tahini, mix the tahini, garlic, and lemon juice to a paste in a bowl. Add some cold water a little at a time to get a runny consistency. Add the salt, parsley or cilantro, and some black pepper and mix well.

Drizzle the kibbeh with the green tahini, and serve with lemon wedges.

Bourekas were traditionally served in the Middle East on Sabbath mornings after the Jews finished praying in synagogue. Introduced to Israel by Bulgarian immigrants in the late 1940s, today they are typically to be found, stuffed with cheese, on just about every street corner and bakery as the ultimate grab-and-go snack. If you make your own, there are so many possibilities when it comes to choosing a sexy filling. These little parcels are a lovely twist on a traditional sandwich and much lighter, too. There are some real flavor bursts going on with this combination of ingredients.

Cumin Potato and Harissa Boureka Sandwich

Makes 4 (or 6) sandwiches

1 sheet of ready-rolled puff pastry
all-purpose flour, for dusting
5 eggs, divided
1 teaspoon nigella seeds
1 teaspoon sesame seeds
1 medium russet potato
1 tablespoon butter
1 tablespoon vegetable or canola oil
½ teaspoon sea salt
½ teaspoon ground cumin
1 teaspoon ground coriander
1 teaspoon fresh lemon juice
2 tablespoons Harissa (*see page 17*)
¼ cup Tahini Dressing (*see page 145*)
handful of herb leaves, such as cilantro, flat-leaf parsley, and mint

Preheat the oven to 425°F and line a large baking pan with nonstick parchment paper.

Unroll the sheet of pastry on a lightly floured board and cut into rectangles measuring 3½ × 5 inches. Place on the lined pan. Beat one of the eggs, then brush it onto the rectangles using a pastry brush. Mix the seeds together in a bowl and sprinkle each pastry rectangle with them. Bake for 25 minutes or until risen and golden.

Meanwhile, cook the potato whole in a saucepan of boiling water for 10 minutes, then drain and let cool slightly.

Cook the remaining 4 eggs in a separate saucepan of boiling water for 7 minutes, then drain and place in a bowl of iced water.

When the potato is cool enough to handle, peel and then slice into ¼-inch thick disks. Heat the butter and oil in a large skillet over medium-high heat, add the potato slices, and sprinkle them with the salt, cumin, and coriander. Fry them for about 4 to 5 minutes on each side until crisp and golden. Add the lemon juice and then transfer the potato slices to a plate.

Shell the eggs and then cut each lengthwise into 4 slices.

To assemble the bourekas, cut each rectangle in half horizontally, being careful not to slice all the way through. Spread ½ tablespoon of harissa on the bottom, then top with a layer of potato and egg slices. Pour some of the tahini dressing over the egg, top with some of the herb leaves, and eat immediately.

Variation

Try substituting eggplant for the potato. Trim a small eggplant, then slice into ¼-inch thick disks, sprinkle both sides lightly with table salt, and let drain in a colander in the sink for 30 minutes. Rinse the salt from the slices and pat dry, then fry in 2 tablespoons vegetable oil until golden. Remove and let drain on paper towels and cool slightly before using to fill the bourekas.

The form of bourekas varies, as do their fillings—bite-sized for canapés, open sandwiches, or made into one large roll and sliced. Grandma Judy makes the best bourekas, simply filled with sharp Cheddar and spinach. Using that as my starting point, I have created some fillings of my own. Although a slightly different take on Grandma Judy's more traditional filling, I've earned her seal of approval with my version, as the earthiness of the chard works really well with the cheeses. But feel free to swap the chard for spinach and the cheeses for any of your preferred choices; it's going to be lovely either way when encased in buttery puff pastry.

Chard, Ricotta, and Parmesan Bourekas

Makes 15 bourekas

For the filling
7oz Swiss chard
table salt
2/3 cup ricotta cheese
¾ cup grated Parmesan cheese
1 egg, beaten
pinch of freshly grated nutmeg
pinch of ground white pepper

For the boureka pastry
1 sheet of ready-rolled puff pastry
all-purpose flour, for dusting
beaten egg, to glaze
2 tablespoons sesame seeds
1 tablespoon nigella seeds

Preheat the oven to 400°F and line 2 baking pans with nonstick parchment paper.

Trim the thick stalks from the Swiss chard and blanch the leaves in a saucepan of salted boiling water for 1 to 2 minutes. Line a sieve with paper towels and then add the chard, pressing down on the leaves with a wooden spoon to remove all the excess water. Let drain and cool, then chop the leaves and combine with the remainder of the filling ingredients.

Unroll the sheet of pastry on a lightly floured work surface and roll out to a further 1 inch all around. Using a 3½-inch square cookie cutter, cut out squares from the pastry—you should get approximately 12 from the sheet. Seal the pastry trimmings in plastic wrap and place in the fridge for rerolling to make more squares later.

Place a heaped tablespoonful of the filling in the center of each square, then brush beaten egg around the border with a pastry brush and fold over to make a triangle. Seal the triangles by pressing down on the edges with the tines of a fork and at the same time making a nice pattern. Place on the lined pans. Reroll and repeat with the chilled pastry trimmings.

Brush each of the triangles liberally with beaten egg (this also helps to prevent the filling from leaking out while baking) and sprinkle with the sesame and nigella seeds.

Bake for 25 to 30 minutes until puffed up and golden. Enjoy hot or cold.

There is no greater marriage than melted cheese and puff pastry and no greater evidence of how much I love this combination than the fact I've stuffed four different types of cheese into these little parcels. The cheese boureka is a classic that needs little else to make it special but the optional twist of red onion and Za'atar suggested here offers a subtle touch of extra flavor.

Four-Cheese Bourekas

Makes 15 bourekas

1 quantity Boureka Pastry (*see* page 36)

For the filling
¾ cup ricotta cheese
¾ cup grated Parmesan cheese
¾ cup crumbled feta cheese
¾ cup grated sharp Cheddar
1 egg
pinch of freshly grated nutmeg
pinch of ground white pepper

Optional extras
½ red onion, minced
2 tablespoons Za'atar (*see* page 15)

Preheat the oven to 400°F and line 2 baking pans with nonstick parchment paper.

Mix all the ingredients for the filling together in a bowl.

Follow the method on page 36 to cut out and fill the boureka pastry with the four-cheese filling, adding some of the red onion and a pinch of the za'atar, if using, then bake. Enjoy hot or cold.

Lox is salmon that has been cured or brined but not smoked, and the dry curing really brings out the flavor of the fish. I was lucky enough to visit New York a few times as a child and to enjoy the typical Jewish delis where lox and cream cheese bagels with pickles were an absolute favorite. Just make sure you purchase a good-quality, thick piece of salmon fillet and remove any bones before starting the curing process.

Lox

Serves 6 to 8

½ cup sea salt
¾ cup granulated sugar
1 teaspoon fennel seeds, crushed
grated zest of ½ lemon
¾ cup black peppercorns
1 package of fresh dill, around 1oz
1¾lb piece of salmon fillet, with skin

Mix the salt, sugar, fennel seeds, grated lemon zest, and peppercorns together in a bowl.

Sprinkle 2 tablespoons of the salt mixture into the bottom of a nonmetallic dish wide enough to hold the salmon and lay 4 or 5 dill sprigs on top. Lightly score the skin of the salmon and then place, skin-side down, on top of the salt mixture and dill. Cover with another 2 tablespoons of the salt mixture or enough to cover. Set the remaining salt mixture aside.

Cover the dish with plastic wrap and let stand in the fridge overnight.

The next day, drain off any liquid from the salmon, then repeat the process by adding 2 tablespoons of the salt mixture to the bottom of the dish and another 2 tablespoons on the top of the salmon to cover. Repeat this process over the following 2 days, replenishing the dill sprigs with fresh ones each time.

On the fifth day, rinse the salt mixture from the salmon really thoroughly and dry with paper towels. Let stand, uncovered, in the fridge overnight to allow the flavors to deepen.

To serve, slice the salmon very thinly starting from the front of the fillet to the tail and serve on a toasted bagel with plenty of cream cheese. Alternatively, forget the cream cheese and smother with Dill and Mustard Sauce (*see* page 29) instead, along with some capers and red onion.

Falafel is ubiquitous across the Middle East and there are numerous ways to make them, but the humble chickpea is always the staple ingredient. Accompanied with a nice runny Tahini Dressing (*see* page 145) and perhaps a dash of chili sauce and hot french fries in doughy warm pitta bread, they are simply heavenly. This is how you will find them served across falafel bars throughout Israel. When you add some succulent white fish as the main ingredient, it lightens them into more of a fishcake texture. They work beautifully with a harissa mayonnaise, perfect for an appetizer or light supper.

Spiced Cod Falafel with Harissa Mayonnaise

Makes about 20 falafel

1 cup dried chickpeas, soaked in cold water overnight

table salt

1¾lb skinless cod loin (or any similar white fish fillet, such as hake or haddock), chopped into large pieces

1 onion, quartered

3 garlic cloves, coarsely chopped

large handful of cilantro, stalks and leaves finely chopped

small handful of dill, stalks and leaves finely chopped

small handful of flat-leaf parsley, stalks and leaves finely chopped

2 teaspoons ground cumin

2 teaspoons ground sumac

pinch of cayenne pepper

¾ cup sesame seeds

2 eggs

1¾ cups panko bread crumbs

freshly ground black pepper

sunflower oil, for deep-frying

sea salt flakes

lemon wedges, for squeezing

For the harissa mayonnaise
1 tablespoon Harissa (*see* page 17)
3 to 4 tablespoons mayonnaise

Drain the chickpeas, rinse, and place in a large saucepan. Cover with plenty of fresh salted water and bring to a boil. Continue to cook for at least 2 hours or until soft, then drain and let cool.

Cut the cod into chunks and add to a food processor along with the cooled chickpeas, onion, garlic, and herbs. Pulse in short bursts so as not to ruin the delicate nature of the fish—a meat grinder works really well here, if you have one. Transfer to a bowl, add the spices, 1 teaspoon table salt (or 2 teaspoons coarse sea salt), a few grindings of black pepper, and the sesame seeds and stir through. Cover and place in the fridge for 30 minutes.

Wet your hands and roll the mixture into walnut-sized balls. Beat the eggs in a bowl and spread the bread crumbs out on a plate. Dip each falafel in turn into the beaten egg and then roll in the bread crumbs.

Preheat the oven to 225°F.

Heat the oil for deep-frying in a deep-fat fryer or large saucepan to around 300°F (don't fill the pan more than halfway). Deep-fry the falafel, in batches, for about 5 to 6 minutes until golden. Remove with a slotted spoon and drain on a plate lined with paper towels, then keep the cooked falafel warm in the oven while you fry the rest.

Meanwhile, mix the harissa with the mayonnaise, adding more or less of each depending on how hot you want it.

Season the falafel with sea salt flakes and serve immediately, accompanied by the harissa mayonnaise and lemon wedges.

Variation

You can omit the coating completely and just fry the falafel as they are to slightly reduce the calories and time involved.

If I see chicken wings on any menu, I order them, as they are my absolute favorite comfort food, and even better when dunked in a creamy garlicky dressing. Aleppo pepper, named after the town in Syria, is also a personal favorite of mine as a seasoning; used frequently throughout the Middle East, it's now slowly making its way on to supermarket shelves in the West. It offers a relatively low-key chile heat with a salty undertone, so I've used it generously in this recipe and avoided additional salt. I've worked for some time on this spice mix and cooking method—baking is so much easier (and less calorific) than deep-frying, and the coating has a killer crunch with a warm, spicy heat.

I have my local Turkish restaurant, which keeps my family happy once a week, to thank for the accompanying sauce. We always order the same thing and I ask for extra of their creamy garlic sauce, as I could pretty much eat it with anything. So when I knew I was doing the book, I thought it was high time I gently persuaded them to give me the recipe.

Crispy Baked Chicken Wings with Aleppo Pepper

Makes around 30 wings

2¼lb chicken wings
1 teaspoon salt
1 teaspoon garlic powder
1 teaspoon lemon pepper
1 teaspoon ground sumac
2 teaspoons Aleppo pepper, plus
1 teaspoon for sprinkling
2 teaspoons smoked paprika
2 teaspoons dried oregano
½ teaspoon English mustard powder
½ teaspoon cayenne pepper
3 teaspoons soft light brown sugar
½ cup all-purpose flour
¾ stick butter, melted

For the creamy garlic sauce
¾ cup full-fat plain yogurt
1 tablespoon mayonnaise
2 teaspoons olive oil, plus extra
if needed
1 garlic clove, crushed
½ teaspoon dried mint
½ teaspoon sea salt, or to taste

Preheat the oven to 425°F. Line a baking pan with a double layer of foil.

Halve the chicken wings at the joint and remove the wing tips, or ask your butcher to do this for you.

Rub the salt into the chicken wings then mix the remaining spices and sugar together in a bowl. Put the flour in a sturdy resealable plastic food bag, add the spice mixture, and then the chicken wings. Seal the bag securely and give it a really good shake to ensure that all the wings are well coated.

Place the chicken wings on the lined pan in a single layer and pour the melted butter over each one, turning them over so that both sides of the wings are covered. Sprinkle with the remaining teaspoon of Aleppo pepper.

Bake for 30 minutes, then turn the wings over and bake for a further 15 minutes until they are crispy and golden and cooked through.

Meanwhile, mix all the ingredients for the creamy garlic sauce together in a bowl and check for seasoning. If it is too thick, thin with a little more olive oil.

Serve the wings hot with the bowl of creamy garlic sauce, or Tahini Dressing (*see* page 145) if you prefer.

This creamy salty dip almost always features at my supper clubs with Matbucha (*see* page 21) and Turkish bread as a sort of rustic amuse bouche; the spiciness of the bell peppers and tomatoes works really well with the feta. I've also served the two together on a crostini for a canapé. This stands up well too as a lovely dip for some crunchy crudités, or you could serve it with a nice beet salad. The possibilities are infinite.

Whipped Feta

Serves 4 generously as part of a meze spread

9oz feta cheese
½ cup Labneh (*see* opposite)
3 tablespoons crème fraîche
1 teaspoon Dijon mustard
2 teaspoons fresh lemon juice
pinch of ground white pepper

Soak the feta in cold water for around 10 minutes. Drain, crumble into a food processor, and blend for a minute or so.

Add the remaining ingredients to the food processor and continue blending until the mixture is smooth, scraping down the sides of the bowl a couple of times to ensure that it is all incorporated.

Transfer the mixture to a bowl, cover, and place in the fridge until you are ready to serve. It will keep, refrigerated, for up to 5 days or so, but I guarantee it won't last that long!

Labneh is the Middle Eastern equivalent of mayonnaise, and the recipe for it is as simple as its one-word title. Tangy and sharp, this cheese is made by straining yogurt and removing the whey. It's a good job that it's so easy to make, as it's highly addictive.

Labneh

Serves 8

2¼lb full-fat plain organic yogurt
1 teaspoon sea salt

To serve
good-quality olive oil
1 to 2 teaspoons Za'atar (*see* page 15)
fresh herbs, such as rosemary, thyme, and tarragon (optional)

Mix the yogurt and salt together, then place in a sieve lined with a large piece of cheesecloth. Bring the 4 corners of the cloth together and secure with some kitchen string or a clip. Suspend the sieve over a deep bowl with enough room between the base of the sieve and bowl to catch all the liquid that drains off the yogurt.

Place in the fridge for a minimum of 6 hours but preferably overnight or up to 48 hours; the longer you leave it to strain, the firmer the labneh will be.

To serve, remove the now-firm labneh from the cloth and place in a bowl. Make a small dip in the top with the back of a spoon. Add some good-quality olive oil and sprinkle with the za'atar.

Alternatively, roll the labneh into balls with lightly oiled hands, place them in a sterilized preserving jar (*see* page 144) with your favorite fresh herbs, and add olive oil to cover. Seal the jar and store in the fridge—the labneh will keep for up to 2 weeks.

Variations

* Try adding 1 to 2 teaspoons ground sumac with the salt at the beginning for a colorful and zingy dip.
* Thin down with fresh lemon juice and add some crushed garlic to make a nice dressing.

This is such a winning combination of flavors and is super easy to prepare. It features on my table at least once a month, usually as a pre-dinner nibble served with some toasted pitta bread.

Artichoke, Spinach, and Pistachio Gratin with Pitta Chips

Serves 6

7oz artichoke hearts in oil from a jar, drained and finely chopped

½ cup finely chopped cooked spinach, (fresh or frozen)

1 cup grated Parmesan cheese, divided

¾ cup soft white or dried bread crumbs, divided

2 fat garlic cloves, crushed

½ cup unsalted pistachio nuts, slightly crushed

½ cup sour cream or crème fraîche

½ cup mayonnaise

freshly ground black pepper

For the pitta chips

3 pieces of pitta bread

2 tablespoons olive oil

freshly picked thyme leaves

sea salt

Preheat the oven to 400°F.

Add the artichokes and spinach to a bowl with half the Parmesan, half the bread crumbs, and all the garlic, pistachio nuts, sour cream or crème fraîche, and mayonnaise. Give everything a good stir, then season generously with black pepper.

Place the mixture in a small gratin dish and top with the remaining Parmesan and bread crumbs.

For the pitta chips, cut the pitta bread into squares and spread them out on a cookie sheet. Brush the olive oil over each square and sprinkle with the thyme leaves and salt.

Bake the gratin for around 20 to 25 minutes, adding the pitta chips to the oven for the final 15 minutes, until both the top of the gratin and the pitta chips are nice and golden. Serve hot or cold.

The closest thing to a good Jewish-style deli in London is The Good Egg in Stoke Newington. While it doesn't do all the classics, it does have one of my favorites, white fish salad, and I am lucky enough to have the recipe. The white fish can be any species of white freshwater fish, which Ashkenazi Jews love to use in cooking (think gefilte fish), that has been smoked. But this may not be easy to get hold of, so unless you are an expert at smoking your own, the method below provides an easy and equally tasty alternative.

White Fish Salad

Serves 6 as part of a meze spread

10½oz white fish fillets
½ teaspoon sea salt
1 teaspoon black peppercorns
3 bay leaves
2 cups milk
6oz cooked smoked trout (smoked haddock will also work well)
6 scallions, very finely sliced

For the mayonnaise
2 egg yolks
1 tablespoon Dijon mustard
1 cup vegetable oil
juice of 1 lemon
½ teaspoon sea salt, if needed
freshly ground black pepper

Put the fish fillets in a nonmetallic dish and sprinkle with the sea salt. Cover and let stand in the fridge overnight.

The next day, rinse the salt from the fish and pat dry. Place in a saucepan with the peppercorns, bay leaves, and milk and simmer gently, uncovered, for 5 minutes. Turn off the heat but leave the fish in the milk for a further 5 minutes. Then transfer the fish to a plate and set aside until cool enough to handle.

Meanwhile, make the mayonnaise. Beat the egg yolks and mustard together in a bowl. Add the oil in a very slow trickle, whisking constantly, until it has all been incorporated and the mayonnaise is nice and thick. Beat in half the lemon juice, then season with the salt, if needed, and black pepper to taste.

Flake the fish into a bowl, then add the smoked trout, scallions, and a generous amount of the mayonnaise. If required, add the remaining lemon juice and some more black pepper.

Serve with a toasted bagel and pickles (*see* pages 142–151).

I would roll anything in dukkah, given the opportunity. These little croquettes were created at one of my supper clubs and have become a regular feature on my menus ever since. There is a good amount of heat in them, so you could always pair them with some plain yogurt lightly seasoned with cumin, or tahini if you don't want a spicy dipping sauce.

Dukkah-crusted Lamb Croquettes with Harissa Ketchup

Makes 12 to 14 croquettes

½ cup panko bread crumbs
¼ cup Dukkah (see page 16)
½ cup all-purpose flour
1 egg
sea salt and freshly ground black pepper
vegetable oil, for deep-frying

For the croquettes
2 tablespoons canola or peanut oil
1 large onion, finely diced
2 garlic cloves, minced
1lb 2oz ground lamb
2 teaspoons ground cumin
2 teaspoons ground coriander
2 teaspoons Lebanese 7-spice Mix (see page 14)
½ teaspoon cayenne pepper
1 teaspoon sea salt

For the harissa ketchup
3 tablespoons tomato ketchup
1 teaspoon Harissa (see page 17), or more if you want it hotter
½ teaspoon ground cumin
1 teaspoon fresh lemon juice

For the croquettes, heat the oil in a skillet, add the onion, and gently fry for 10 minutes until lightly golden. Add the garlic and cook for a further 2 minutes, then let cool.

Mix the cooled onion and garlic with the lamb and all the remaining croquette ingredients, then shape into small cylinders about 2 inches long.

Add the panko and the dukkah to a food processor, if you have one, and pulse a few times to combine and make the crumbs slightly finer. Alternatively, place in a sturdy resealable plastic food bag, seal securely, and crush with a rolling pin. Spread the mixture out on a plate. Season the flour with salt and black pepper and spread out on a separate plate. Beat the egg in a bowl.

Roll the lamb cylinders in the seasoned flour, then dip in the beaten egg, and finally coat with the bread-crumb mixture. Let chill in the fridge for a minimum of 30 minutes.

Meanwhile, mix all the ingredients for the harissa ketchup together in a bowl and set aside. Preheat the oven to 225°F.

Heat the oil for deep-frying in a deep-fat fryer or medium saucepan (make sure that the oil is a minimum of 3 inches deep, but don't fill the pan more than halfway) to around 340°F. Check the oil temperature by dropping in a bread crumb; when it sizzles, the oil is ready. Reduce the heat to medium and fry the croquettes in batches, being careful not to overcrowd the pan, for 5 to 7 minutes until they are crisp and golden. Remove with a slotted spoon and drain on a plate lined with paper towels. Keep the cooked croquettes hot in the oven while you fry the rest.

Serve the croquettes hot, sprinkled with sea salt, and with the bowl of harissa ketchup on the side.

Mahkuda is an Algerian dish that my mother-in-law Judith's mother, Safta, would cook up all the time and now my mother-in-law makes during High Holidays. I've taken the same ingredients but constructed it as more of a traditional tortilla-style dish, which works well served either hot or cold, with a crisp salad or some cooked meats. The addition of the cumin and harissa makes it earthy and warming with a gentle kick.

Mahkuda with Harissa

Serves 8

6 to 7 round red or round white potatoes

1 large or 2 medium onions, minced

1¼ cups olive oil, divided

6 large eggs

2 tablespoons Harissa (see page 17), or more if you want it hotter

1 teaspoon ground cumin

sea salt and freshly ground black pepper

Peel the potatoes, then cut in half vertically, and slice each half thinly so that you have half-moon shapes; use a mandoline slicer if you have one.

Add the potatoes to a large bowl with the onion, season with salt, and mix together to combine.

Heat all but 1 tablespoon of the oil in a nonstick skillet over high heat. Check the oil temperature by adding a potato; if it sizzles, the oil is hot enough. Turn the heat down to medium and add the rest of the potatoes and onion. Cook for 20 minutes in total, turning the ingredients over very carefully in the oil every 5 minutes, or until the potatoes are soft all the way through—you don't want to fry the ingredients too quickly.

Drain the potatoes in a sieve over a bowl, reserving the oil—this has so much flavor, so you absolutely must keep it for other uses.

Beat the eggs in a large bowl, then mix in the harissa and cumin. Season again with salt and some black pepper and then add the drained potatoes and onion. Mix very gently to avoid breaking up the potatoes.

Heat the remaining tablespoon of oil in the same skillet, add the egg and potato mixture, and cook for around 4 to 5 minutes—you want the heat medium-low here to avoid burning the bottom. Place a plate larger than the diameter of the skillet on top and very carefully invert the skillet to turn the mahkuda over onto the plate. Then return the mahkuda to the pan to cook the other side, adding in any potato that's escaped. Tuck the edges in with a spatula, if need be, to make a nice shape.

Cook for a further 3 minutes and then repeat the turning process as before, placing the plate on top and inverting the skillet. The result should be a lovely golden mahkuda. Serve warm.

Tip

Feel free to be creative here and add olives, bell peppers, and any other Mediterranean ingredients you feel are appropriate.

There is nothing more comforting than the smell of fried food, except my mom really didn't like the smell of it in the house, so we enjoyed the pleasure of this recipe only once a year on Yom Kippur. She would make the fish balls the day before, partly so that the smell would dissipate before the guests arrived but mainly because traditionally you are meant to have done all your cooking before the 25-hour fast comes in and these are designed to be served cold. I cook these for almost every High Holiday as part of a buffet spread with Egg and Onion (*see* page 62), Chopped Liver (*see* page 63), and Hungarian Cucumber Salad (*see* page 180). Ask your fish dealer to grind the fish for you in advance—that way you don't have to worry about picking out the bones and processing it yourself.

Fried Fish Balls

Makes about 45 balls

1 large carrot
1 onion
2¼ lb ground white fish
1 egg, beaten
2 tablespoons medium matzo meal
2 teaspoons granulated sugar
½ tablespoon sea salt, or to taste
freshly ground black pepper
2 quarts corn oil, for deep-frying

To serve
mayonnaise
lemon wedges

Peel and grate the carrot and onion; use the grating attachment on your food processor if you have one.

Put the ground fish in a large bowl and add the carrot and onion along with the egg, matzo meal, sugar, salt, and some black pepper, mixing well with your hands until everything is incorporated.

Heat the oil for deep-frying in a deep-fat fryer or large saucepan (don't fill the pan more than halfway) to around 340°F. Take a small walnut-sized amount of the fish mixture and, using a slotted spoon, drop it carefully into the oil. Cook for 7 to 8 minutes until it is a deep golden brown. Taste for seasoning and adjust if necessary, then shape the rest of the mixture into ping-pong-sized balls. Fry the fish balls in batches, ensuring that they cook for a minimum of 7 minutes so that the inside is cooked through. Remove with a slotted spoon and drain on a platter lined with paper towels.

Let cool completely before serving or, even better, make the day before, then cover and chill until required.

Serve with mayonnaise and lemon wedges, for squeezing.

Schmear, better known as flavored cream cheese, is such a lovely, simple spread for toasted bagels or crispy *lavash* crackers. I've classically paired mine with smoked salmon, but added some baked salmon to lighten it a little, along with plenty of fresh lemon juice and dill. Try experimenting with other flavorings of your choice; with a base of rich, creamy cheese, you can't go too far wrong.

Poached and Smoked Salmon Schmear

Serves 6 to 8

5½oz piece of salmon fillet
1²⁄₃ cups full-fat cream cheese
¼lb smoked salmon, chopped
juice of ½ lemon, or to taste
1 teaspoon sea salt
plenty of freshly ground black pepper
2 tablespoons freshly chopped dill
toasted bagels, to serve

Preheat the oven to 400°F.

Wrap the salmon fillet in foil, place on a baking pan, and bake for 8 minutes. The salmon should be almost cooked, but you want it to be a tiny bit pink in the middle. Let cool, then remove the skin, if it has some, and check for any stray bones.

Put the cream cheese in a food processor and blend well, scraping down the sides every now and then to ensure that it is all fully blended. Add the smoked salmon, salmon fillet, and lemon juice and blend again so that all the ingredients are combined; it is okay to retain some texture in the salmon.

Transfer to a bowl, season with the salt and black pepper, and add the chopped dill. Check for seasoning and add more lemon juice if required.

Serve with toasted bagels.

One of my favorite Friday night dinners is when we start with Egg and Onion and Chopped Liver (*see* opposite) with Challah (*see* page 204); it never fails to take me back to my childhood. I've offered two variations here, the second a kosher option if eating with a meat meal, replacing the mayonnaise with oil as the binding agent, to make a more traditional recipe in the Jewish diaspora.

Egg and Onion, Two Ways

Serves 8 as part
of a meze spread

Way One

10 eggs
4 scallions, very finely sliced
2 tablespoons good-quality full-fat mayonnaise
sea salt and ground white pepper
a few finely snipped chives, to garnish (optional)

Put the eggs in a saucepan of water and bring to a boil. Then turn off the heat and let stand for 7 minutes. Drain the eggs, add to cold water, and set aside until cool enough to handle, then shell.

Place the shelled eggs in a bowl and use a potato masher to chop the eggs as finely as you would like, or use the large holes of a box grater.

Transfer to a serving bowl with the scallions and mayonnaise, season to taste with salt and white pepper, and stir well to combine. Scatter with the chives just before serving, if you like.

Tip

For a nice little twist, mix a teaspoon of Dijon mustard into the mayonnaise before adding it to the egg.

Way Two

10 eggs
¾ cup vegetable oil
3 large white onions, finely diced
½ teaspoon sweet paprika
sea salt and ground white pepper

Cook, shell, and grate the eggs as above, then place in a serving bowl.

Heat the oil in a large skillet, add the onions, and gently fry for around 25 minutes until golden brown.

Using a slotted spoon to avoid adding excess oil, spoon the fried onions onto the eggs, and mix them in. Add a little more oil if needed to bind the mixture together. Add the paprika and season to taste with salt and white pepper, then cover and chill in the fridge until ready to serve.

Chopped liver is a very popular appetizer served on the Sabbath and High Holidays, most typically with a bowl of Egg and Onion next to it (*see* opposite). It's rich and super high in fat and calories, but we forgive it because it tastes so good and everything in moderation, as they say. Traditional recipes call for the use of *schmaltz* (rendered chicken fat) as the binding agent, but vegetable oil is a perfectly acceptable substitute, and besides, I've already strayed quite far from the norm with this twist on a classic.

Chopped Liver

Serves 6 as part of a meze spread

¼ cup vegetable oil, divided
14oz chicken livers
1 large onion, finely diced
⅓ cup Madeira wine
sea salt and freshly ground black pepper
1 hard-boiled egg, shelled and grated (optional)

Heat half the oil in a skillet over medium-high heat. Pat the livers dry, and when the oil is hot, add them to the skillet and stand back; they will spatter and spit. Turn the heat down slightly and let the livers fry, undisturbed, for 3 minutes, then turn them over and cook for a further 2 minutes before transferring them to a plate.

Heat the remaining oil in the same skillet, add the onion, and cook for around 10 minutes until it caramelizes a little. Then turn the heat to its highest setting, add the Madeira, and let it cook until it has reduced completely and there is almost no liquid left; this will take no more than 5 minutes.

Drain off any juice collected from the livers and then add them to a food processor with the onion mixture. Season generously with salt and black pepper and blend for a few seconds—you want to retain a little texture.

Transfer to a bowl and check for seasoning, then cover and chill in the fridge for a minimum of 6 hours or up to 2 days.

To serve the liver, smear generously on Challah (*see* page 204) or crackers, topped with the grated egg, if you like.

Tip

Prepare this recipe the day before if you have the time, as the flavor will intensify overnight.

Soups

Known as "Jewish penicillin," this soup is loved by Jews all around the world and there is always a healthy debate about how to cook it best. My mother will forgive me for adapting this slightly. In fact, it was she who recommended I substitute the whole chicken for thighs—they seem to impart so much more flavor, plus the meat remains edible even after the three hours' cooking time. The *kneidlach*, which translates from the Yiddish to "dumpling," or better known to many as matzah balls, are tasty white fluffy balls that go hand in hand with this soup. You need only patience for this soup; there is very little hard work for an end result that is both comforting and delicious—and, as some would argue, medicinal.

Mommy's Golden Chicken Soup with Kneidlach

Serves 10

8 large chicken thighs, about 2lb

4 quarts boiling water

2 large onions, unpeeled and halved

6 large carrots, peeled and halved

1 large leek, trimmed, cleaned, and chopped

1 small rutabaga, peeled and chopped

2 turnips, peeled and quartered

3 celery stalks, with leaves, chopped

¼ cup chicken stock powder or 4 chicken stock cubes

1½ tablespoons sea salt

10 black peppercorns

4 bay leaves

Osem mini croutons, to serve

For the kneidlach (makes 20 balls)

1 cup medium matzo meal

½ teaspoon table salt, or to taste

¼ teaspoon ground white pepper

1 teaspoon baking powder

¼ teaspoon garlic powder

3 eggs

3 tablespoons vegetable oil

Optional extras

1 tablespoon chicken stock powder or 1 chicken stock cube

1 teaspoon table salt

Put the chicken thighs in a large saucepan and add the boiled water. Simmer over medium heat for a few minutes, allowing the fat to rise to the surface before skimming it off. Then add all the vegetables, the stock powder or cubes, salt, peppercorns, and bay leaves. Reduce the heat to a slow simmer and let the soup gently bubble away for 3 hours.

In the meantime, make the kneidlach. Mix the matzo meal, salt, white pepper, baking powder, and garlic powder together in a bowl. Beat the eggs with the oil, add to the matzo meal mixture, and stir through with a fork until just combined. Cover and chill in the fridge for 30 minutes to firm up, or overnight if you are preparing the soup a day ahead.

Remove the chicken from the soup with a slotted spoon, transfer to a bowl, and let cool slightly. Strain the soup over a large saucepan. Remove the carrots, turnips, and rutabaga and set aside; discard the rest of the vegetables. Check for seasoning and add more salt if needed (if you are making ahead, adjust the seasoning when you reheat the soup, as the flavor will intensify).

With damp hands, roll the chilled kneidlach mixture into walnut-sized balls. If cooking the kneidlach in the chicken soup, reheat the soup, and when it is starting to come to a boil, drop in the balls and let simmer gently for around 25 to 30 minutes or until light and fluffy and cooked through. Alternatively, to cook the kneidlach separately, bring a large saucepan of water to a boil with the optional extras. Add the matzo balls one by one, cover the pan with the lid, and simmer over low heat for 25 to 30 minutes until cooked through. Drain and add to a bowl until you are ready to serve the soup.

To serve, pull the skin away from the chicken, and remove the bone along with any gristle. Tear the chicken into bite-sized pieces. Cut the reserved vegetables into bite-sized pieces and place in the bottom of your soup bowls with some chicken and 2 kneidlach per serving. Ladle the golden broth on top and serve scattered with mini croutons.

My sister Debbie served this to me as a dinner party appetizer one night and it was so delicious; even better, it's very healthy. I've recreated it many times since and it works just as well as a filling and virtuous lunch with some lovely dense rye bread or sourdough as it does as a no-fuss dinner party offering. I threw in some leftover cooked chickpeas at the end once and now I always add them—aside from providing some welcome texture to the soup, they also make it into more of a meal in itself.

I would urge you to use really good-quality organic canned cherry tomatoes for this soup and not be tempted to substitute other types of canned tomatoes; only fresh would be an acceptable alternative.

Debbie's Cherry Tomato, Red Lentil, and Chickpea Soup

Serves 8

2 white onions

6 carrots

2 celery stalks

3 garlic cloves

olive oil, for sautéeing

1 cup dried red lentils

3 × 14oz cans cherry tomatoes

1½ quarts chicken or vegetable stock

3 bay leaves

a few sprigs of thyme

¼ cup dried chickpeas, soaked and cooked or 14oz can chickpeas, drained and rinsed

sea salt and freshly ground black pepper

dollop of crème fraîche (optional)

Peel and finely chop the onions, carrots, celery, and garlic, or add to your food processor and pulse until everything is nice and small but not puréed.

Add a few glugs of olive oil to a large saucepan, add the vegetables, and sauté over medium heat for about 10 minutes until they are soft.

Rinse the lentils well until the water runs clear and then add to the saucepan and cook for a minute. Stir in the canned tomatoes and stock and bring to a boil. Add the bay leaves and thyme and season to taste with salt and black pepper. Turn the heat down, cover with a lid, and simmer gently for around 35 to 40 minutes.

When the soup is ready, it will be nice and thick. At this point, you can either blend completely until smooth using a stick blender or by transferring to a blender, or partially blend to keep it thick and chunky.

Add the chickpeas to the soup and continue cooking until they are heated through. Check and adjust the seasoning, then serve with a dollop of crème fraîche if you like.

I absolutely love Jerusalem artichokes—they are so versatile and delicious. The only problem is that the season for them is fairly short, so I tend to find myself making large quantities of soups and purées and stashing them away in the freezer so that I can readily get my fix. The addition of hazelnuts elevates this soup to an ultra-rich and decadent dish, making it a perfect trouble-free appetizer that can easily be doubled in quantity to feed a small crowd.

Jerusalem Artichoke Soup with Toasted Hazelnuts

Serves 4

2 tablespoons olive oil
2 tablespoons butter
3 banana shallots, minced
2 celery stalks, finely chopped
1 fat garlic clove, minced
1lb 10oz Jerusalem artichokes, scrubbed and chopped
1 bay leaf
1 teaspoon wild dried thyme
1 quart hot chicken or vegetable stock
¾ cup blanched hazelnuts
2 tablespoons crème fraîche
juice of ½ lemon
sea salt and freshly ground black pepper

Heat the oil and the butter in a saucepan, add the shallots and celery, and cook for a few minutes until they are starting to soften. Add the garlic and continue to cook for a couple more minutes.

Add the Jerusalem artichokes, bay leaf, and thyme, season with salt and black pepper, and cook for a minute before adding the hot stock. Cover the pan with a lid and simmer for 20 minutes until the artichokes are nice and tender.

Heat a dry skillet over medium heat, add the hazelnuts, and toast for around 5 minutes, shaking the pan every so often to ensure that they don't burn. Tip them onto a plate.

Remove the bay leaf from the soup and add about three-quarters of the hazelnuts, chopping the remainder of the nuts and reserving. Blend the soup with a stick blender until smooth, or transfer to a blender to blend. Add the crème fraîche and blend again.

Squeeze the lemon juice over the top, ladle the soup into serving bowls, and scatter with the reserved chopped hazelnuts.

Legumes are a mainstay of my kitchen cupboard. I grew up eating hearty dishes heavily laden with them and now I too find myself cooking with them frequently. This soup should be nice and thick, and the addition of turkey bacon slices makes it a complete meal in a bowl. Serve with a generous amount of crusty bread.

Split Pea and Vegetable Soup

Serves 6

2 tablespoons vegetable or canola oil

5½oz turkey bacon, thinly sliced

2 onions, minced

6 carrots, finely chopped

2 celery stalks, finely chopped

2 garlic cloves, crushed

1¼ cups dried green split peas, soaked in cold water overnight

1½ quarts vegetable or chicken stock

2 bay leaves

sea salt and freshly ground black pepper

Heat the oil in a large saucepan, add the turkey bacon, and fry for a couple of minutes until they start to color. Add the onions, carrots, celery, and garlic and cook over medium heat for around 5 minutes until the vegetables have softened.

Drain and rinse the split peas, then add to the pan, stirring them into the vegetables, and cover with the stock. Add the bay leaves, some salt (go easy if you are using stock powder), and a few generous grindings of black pepper.

Bring the soup to a simmer, then cover with a lid and cook for around 2 to 2½ hours or until the peas are soft. You may need to add some water to the pan if the soup is too thick.

Pour half the soup out and blend with a stick blender, or transfer to a blender to blend. Return to the rest of the soup, stir to combine, and serve.

Big plates with meat & fish

A true *shawarma* consists of heavily spiced meat cooked on a spit, being turned slowly for hours and hours before slivers of the juicy meat are piled high in warm flatbreads with other delicious accompaniments. This is my take on a home-style shawarma, so it's quick and easy to cook yet packed full of flavor. The blend of the peppery cardamom with the warm cinnamon and allspice in the Lebanese spice mix is a marriage made in heaven when it meets a chicken thigh. Try serving this with Sephardi Rice with Vermicelli and Lentils (*see* page 155) and Israeli "Chik Chak" Salad (*see* page 172), or pile onto some flatbread with chili sauce.

Chicken Shawarma with Jerusalem and Lebanese Spices

Serves 4

6 boneless, skinless chicken thighs
1 teaspoon ground turmeric
1 teaspoon ground coriander
½ teaspoon ground cardamom
2 heaped teaspoons Lebanese 7-spice Mix (*see* page 14)
2 tablespoons olive oil, plus extra for frying if preferred
sea salt

To serve
grilled flatbreads
Israeli "Chik Chak" Salad (*see* page 172)
chili sauce
pickled peppers

Start by laying each chicken thigh in turn between 2 sheets of plastic wrap and flattening with a meat mallet or rolling pin until they are approximately an even thickness of around ½ inch throughout.

Add the spices to a bowl and stir in the olive oil to make a paste.

Place the chicken in a sturdy resealable plastic food bag with the spice paste, seal securely, and squish it all together until it is well coated. Place in the fridge for as long as you can to marinate; a minimum of 1 hour, but overnight is preferable.

Heat a nonstick skillet until smoking; there is enough oil on the chicken not to warrant adding any to the skillet, but feel free to if you prefer. Add the chicken to the hot skillet and fry over high heat for about 2 minutes, then turn the heat down to medium and cook for a further 3 minutes, or until it has a good deep color. Turn the chicken over and fry on the other side for another 5 minutes. The thickness of the chicken will determine how long it needs, so use your judgment and check to make sure there is no pink left—there is a fine line between nicely charred and burnt, so keep a close eye on it.

Serve immediately, cut into slices, with grilled flatbreads, chili sauce, and pickled peppers.

The food memories that evoke the strongest feeling of nostalgia are my mom's Friday night roast chicken with onions and really crispy roast potatoes. It was the one night of the week when we all ate together as a family, and it marked the start of the weekend and being able to stay up late. (Remember *Golden Girls* and *Cheers* anyone?). I would race to the pan before it got washed to scrape up the burnt-on bits of onion and roast potato, and while you eventually have to deal with the consequences of that degree of crispiness while doing the dishes, those delicious morsels are more than worth it. Besides, you are only using one pan. This is such a simple supper with nothing fancy about it, perhaps too simple even to constitute a recipe, but more of a way of celebrating the flavor of one of the most ubiquitous *carne* in the Jewish culinary canon.

Friday Night Chicken with Onions and Roast Potatoes

Serves 6

3 onions, thickly sliced

1 free-range chicken, around 4½lb

6 large russet potatoes, peeled and cut into whatever shape you like your roast potatoes to be

3 tablespoons olive oil

1 teaspoon sea salt

freshly ground black pepper

green salad, to serve (optional)

Preheat the oven to 400°F.

Place the onions in your roasting pan—you want one large enough to hold all the potatoes too. Set the chicken on top, breast-side down, and dot the potatoes all around it. Smear the olive oil generously all over the chicken and the onions and potatoes, and season with the salt and plenty of black pepper.

Roast for 1 hour 45 minutes, turning the potatoes and onions over in the oil and chicken juices every 25 minutes. Turn the chicken breast-side up to crisp up the skin for the last 30 minutes of the cooking time.

Serve with a green salad, if liked.

Note

Some people prefer to parboil the potatoes first in salted water, but the long cooking time here means that the potatoes cook just as well without this step and turn lovely and crisp.

During *MasterChef*, we were set a brief of choosing someone who inspired us and creating a dish around that person. It was a no-brainer for me; I had to do something with roast chicken, inspired by my mom, but it had to be elevated from the classic bird I knew and loved into a *MasterChef*-worthy creation. This recipe incorporates all my favorite spices. With an hour to cook this dish, I spatchcocked a squab chicken to allow it to cook faster, but to eliminate the need for any butchery here, I've recreated the recipe using thighs, although it would work with any part of the chicken or, of course, the entire bird. Not only is it very easy to make, it is ridiculously tasty and fit for either a simple family supper or as part of a more elaborate banquet.

Baharat Spiced Chicken

Serves 6

12 bone-in, skin-on chicken thighs

2 red onions, thinly sliced

2 tablespoons baharat

2 teaspoons ground sumac

1 teaspoon ground cumin

1 teaspoon ground coriander

4 preserved lemons, halved, flesh scooped out and discarded

3 garlic cloves, crushed

1¾ cups chicken stock (using 1 tablespoon chicken stock powder)

3 tablespoons olive oil

1 teaspoon sea salt

a few grinds of black pepper

rice or couscous, to serve

Add the chicken thighs to a large, sturdy resealable plastic food bag with all the other ingredients, then seal securely before massaging the bag to mix everything together. Let marinate in the fridge for a minimum of 2 hours but preferably overnight.

Preheat the oven to 400°F.

Add the chicken and all the remaining contents of the bag to a roasting pan and roast for 45 to 50 minutes until the chicken is golden brown and the juices run clear when pierced with a knife.

Serve the chicken with a generous amount of the onions and lemon skins over rice or couscous, ladling the juices on top.

When I found out that I was going to be a contestant on *MasterChef*, I called my husband's cousin Michal in Israel for some help with recipes. She is a very gifted cook with an effortless, down-to-earth style that's reflected in her hospitality. Having been fortunate enough to have sat as a guest at her table, I knew I could trust her. This is an adaptation of her recipe, and while it didn't make the *MasterChef* table for fear of its simplicity, it works beautifully well as a dinner party dish or on a celebration table, in particular for Rosh Hashanah, given its sweet notes and honey.

Sweet Honey Chicken

Serves 6

6 skin-on chicken leg quarters or 12 bone-in, skin-on chicken thighs, or a mixture of thighs and drumsticks

12 shallots, peeled but left whole

3 sweet potatoes, scrubbed and cut into wedges

2 bay leaves

5 sprigs of thyme

12 Medjool dates, pitted

sea salt and freshly ground black pepper

rice or couscous, to serve

½ cup toasted sliced almonds, to garnish

For the sauce

⅓ cup liquid honey

⅓ cup soy sauce

3 tablespoons balsamic vinegar

2 tablespoons olive oil

¾-inch piece of fresh ginger root, peeled and grated

3 garlic cloves, crushed

2 cinnamon sticks

1 tablespoon ground coriander

1¼ cups red wine

Preheat the oven to 350°F.

Place the chicken, skin-side up, on a baking pan and arrange the shallots and sweet potato wedges around the chicken.

Mix all the ingredients for the sauce together and pour evenly over the chicken and vegetables, ensuring that everything is well covered. Season generously with salt and black pepper, then tuck in the bay leaves and thyme sprigs.

Cover the pan with foil and roast for 30 minutes.

Turn the oven up to 400°F and remove the foil. Add the dates and give all the ingredients around the chicken a good stir in the sauce, then cook, uncovered, for a further 30 minutes until the chicken is nicely golden and everything has slightly caramelized.

Serve the chicken over a bowl of rice or couscous with lots of the sauce, scattered with the sliced almonds to garnish.

These chicken meatballs really pack a flavor punch. Quick, simple to prepare, and healthy, they need nothing more than some plain rice or a fresh salad to accompany them, making for an easy lunch or dinner.

Chicken and Pistachio Meatballs with Cilantro Tahini

Serves 6; makes 25 meatballs

For the meatballs
½ onion
⅔ cup unsalted pistachio nuts
½ cup medium matzo meal
handful of tarragon leaves
2 handfuls of cilantro, leaves and stalks
2 handfuls of flat-leaf parsley, leaves and stalks
1 tablespoon fresh lime juice
2 teaspoons ground cumin
2 teaspoons ground coriander
1 teaspoon dried red chile flakes
1 teaspoon sea salt
½ teaspoon freshly ground black pepper
1lb 2oz ground chicken
1 egg, beaten
2 tablespoons olive oil, divided

For the cilantro tahini
2 large handfuls of cilantro leaves
1 garlic clove, crushed
¼ cup tahini
juice of 1 lemon
pinch of sea salt

To serve
steamed rice
seeds from ½ pomegranate
handful of mint leaves, finely chopped

Add all the meatball ingredients except the chicken, egg, and oil to a food processor and pulse until the mixture comes together; you want a coarse, grainy consistency.

Transfer to a large bowl and add the chicken and the egg, working the mixture together with your hands just until it is combined; you don't want to overwork it. Cover and place in the fridge for 30 minutes.

Meanwhile, clean out the food processor, then add all the ingredients for the cilantro tahini to it and blend. With the motor running, slowly add some water until you have a loose dressing with the consistency of heavy cream. Transfer to bowl, cover, and refrigerate until needed.

Preheat the oven to 425°F.

Wet your hands and roll the chicken mixture into ping-pong-sized balls. Grease a baking dish large enough to hold the meatballs in a single layer with 1 tablespoon of the olive oil. Brush the remaining tablespoon of oil over the top of the meatballs and bake for 15 minutes.

Serve the meatballs on a bed of steamed rice garnished with the pomegranate seeds and the chopped mint, drizzled generously with the cilantro tahini.

One of the highlights of my trip to Jordan (and there were many) was cooking in the town of Ajloun at the house of Um Hamzeh, a wonderful Palestinian woman who welcomed us graciously into her kitchen. I watched her make this dish, then sat and greedily devoured the result of her hard work—so much flavor from a few simple ingredients. The key is using really good-quality sumac—preferably Turkish, if you can get it—as this is the star of the show. The bread is important too; the large round naan bread they sell in Turkish and Middle Eastern grocery stores are thick enough to withstand the cooking process. While this recipe looks like a long process, at the end you have a spectacular, showstopping dish for the center of the table for everyone to tear and share.

"Musakhan" Sumac Chicken

Serves 6 to 8

12 chicken drumsticks and thighs

2 tablespoons mild curry powder, plus 1 teaspoon, divided

2 cups olive oil, plus 3 tablespoons, divided

2 teaspoons sea salt, divided

2 tablespoons pomegranate molasses

3 large onions, finely diced

2 garlic cloves, minced

1 teaspoon freshly ground black pepper

2 cups chicken stock

½ cup ground sumac, divided

6 large round naan or taboon breads

To garnish

1 tablespoon olive oil

½ cup sliced almonds (or use slivered almonds)

Preheat the oven to 400°F. Place the chicken on a baking pan. Mix the 2 tablespoons of curry powder with the 3 tablespoons of olive oil. Use a pastry brush to spread the mixture all over each piece of chicken, then sprinkle with half the salt. Bake the chicken for 35 minutes.

Remove the chicken from the oven and drain the juice into a pitcher, but leave the chicken in the pan. Brush the pomegranate molasses all over the chicken and return to the oven for a further 20 minutes until the top is golden and crispy and the chicken is cooked through.

While the chicken is cooking, add the onions to a large saucepan with the remaining curry powder, the garlic, black pepper, and remaining teaspoon of salt and stir over high heat, without oil, for 5 minutes. Cover the pan with a lid, turn the heat down to medium, and cook for a further 10 minutes, stirring occasionally. Add the remaining 2 cups of oil, the chicken stock, reserved juices from the chicken pan, and 2 tablespoons of the sumac. Let the mixture boil gently for about 5 to 7 minutes until the onions are soft.

Cut each bread round into 6 triangles. Using tongs, carefully dunk each triangle into the onion and oil mixture, then place the bread in a single layer in a large, flat, shallow ovenproof paella-style pan. Using a slotted spoon, lift out some onions and spread them over each piece of bread. Then take 2 tablespoons of the sumac and sprinkle it over the top. Bake the bread for 8 to 10 minutes until it has started to crisp. Repeat the entire process until you have used up all the bread and have 3 layers. Once all the bread has been baked, place the chicken pieces on top and return to the oven for 5 minutes to heat through.

Meanwhile, for the garnish, heat the oil in a skillet over medium heat, add the almonds, and fry, stirring constantly, until starting to turn golden, then immediately transfer to a plate.

Remove the chicken from the oven and scatter it with the almonds. Serve immediately with plenty of napkins.

The ubiquitous Ashkenazi feel-good food, schnitzel deserves to be on the highest of pedestals. When I went through a typical teenage phase of deciding to be a vegetarian, my mom gave me a week to cave, and when I showed no sign of weakening, she decided to cook schnitzel. Needless to say, the confirmed carnivore I am today can easily be traced back to that one particular mealtime. Bugga, my father-in-law, makes a killer schnitzel, so I have dedicated this recipe to him. Marinating the meat overnight in egg and garlic is not a conventional method, but it really helps to tenderize the meat as well as imparting a lovely flavor. I grew up with the matzo meal crumb, but love the crispier crunch of panko, so I leave the choice up to you.

Bugga's Turkey Schnitzel

Serves 4

4 boneless turkey breast steaks
3 eggs
1 teaspoon sweet paprika
2 garlic cloves, crushed
1½ cups panko bread crumbs (or substitute ¾ cup medium matzo meal)
sunflower oil, for shallow-frying
sea salt and freshly ground black pepper

To serve
Israeli "Chik Chak" Salad (optional, *see* page 172)
lemon wedges

Lay each turkey breast steak in turn between 2 sheets of plastic wrap and, using a meat mallet or rolling pin, lightly pound the meat until it is around ¼ inch thick.

Beat the eggs in a large, shallow dish wide enough to hold the turkey steaks in a single layer, then add the paprika and crushed garlic and season generously with salt and black pepper. Roll the turkey steaks in the mixture to coat, cover the dish with plastic wrap, and let marinate in the fridge for at least 2 hours but preferably overnight.

Spread the panko bread crumbs (or matzo meal) onto a large plate, then coat each turkey steak in turn evenly with the crumbs.

Heat a skillet with a thin film of oil—you want a depth of around ½ inch. Test if the oil is hot enough by dropping in a bread crumb; when it sizzles, the oil is ready. Fry the turkey steaks over medium heat for approximately 4 minutes on each side until golden brown, turning them over once.

Transfer to a plate lined with paper towels or, if not serving immediately, set them on a baking pan lined with foil and place in an oven preheated to 225°F to keep warm.

Season the schnitzel with sea salt and serve with Israeli "Chik Chak" Salad, if liked, and lemon wedges.

This is definitely a special occasion dish and one that I constructed to secure a place in the semifinals of *MasterChef*. I experimented with lots of different seasonings, but was most proud of my own black za'atar invention, which adds a really interesting flavor to the meat. Be careful when scoring the duck skin so that you cut deep enough to render the fat, but not so deep that you penetrate the meat, which can cause it to toughen when cooking.

Seared Duck Breast with a Black Za'atar Crust and Braised Puy Lentils

Serves 2

2 tablespoons black sesame seeds
2 tablespoons fennel seeds
1 teaspoon cumin seeds
2 teaspoons dried red chile flakes
1 tablespoon ground sumac
½ teaspoon ground cinnamon
1 teaspoon freshly picked thyme leaves
2 duck breasts
2 tablespoons date syrup
sea salt and freshly ground black pepper

For the lentils
1 cup chicken or beef stock
2 teaspoons duck fat
1 banana shallot, finely chopped
1 leek, white part only, trimmed, cleaned, and finely chopped
2 tablespoons tomato paste
²/₃ cup dried Puy lentils, rinsed and drained
3 sprigs of thyme
1 garlic clove, peeled but kept whole
2 tablespoons crème fraîche (optional)
sea salt and freshly ground black pepper

Start by making the spiced crust for the duck breast. Heat a dry skillet over medium heat, add the black sesame, fennel, and cumin seeds and lightly toast, shaking the pan constantly. Add the mixture to a mortar and pestle, crush, and then place in a bowl with the remaining spices, thyme, and some salt and black pepper.

Pat the duck breasts dry. Using a sharp knife, score the skin in a crisscross pattern. Brush the skin of each of the breasts with the date syrup and then pat about a tablespoonful of the spice mixture on top, rubbing it in to make sure that the skin is well coated. Place in a dish, cover, and let marinate in the fridge for up to an hour.

For the lentils, heat the stock in a saucepan. In a separate saucepan, melt the duck fat, add the shallot and leek, and cook, stirring, for about 3 minutes until soft. Add the tomato paste and the lentils and cook for a further minute to coat before adding the thyme, garlic, and hot stock. Bring to a boil, then reduce to a simmer. Cover the pan and cook, stirring occasionally, for 30 to 40 minutes until soft but still retaining a bite and the liquid has evaporated; top off with a little hot water if the lentils need more cooking time. Discard the garlic and thyme, season with salt and black pepper, and let rest in the saucepan, covered, while you cook the duck.

Preheat the oven to 425°F.

Place the duck breasts, skin-side down, in a cold, preferably ovenproof skillet without any oil over medium heat for around 6 to 8 minutes or until the skin is golden brown. Pour off the excess fat and then flip the duck breasts over and cook on the flesh side for a minute to seal. If your pan is ovenproof, transfer to the oven, or transfer the duck breasts to a baking pan, skin-side up, and cook for a further 10 minutes for medium rare, 12 minutes for medium, or 15 minutes for well done.

Remove the duck from the oven and let rest; it will need a good 5 minutes at least. Meanwhile, add the crème fraîche to the lentils, if using, and stir through. To serve, carve the duck into slices. Place a few spoonfuls of the lentils on the plates and top with the slices of duck.

I have had the pleasure of sharing a sofa with the incredible Claudia Roden on a panel discussing the wonders of Sephardi cuisine. One of the greatest ambassadors of Jewish world cuisine out there today, she has been writing cookbooks for more than 60 years, and her *A Book of Middle Eastern Food*, first published in 1968 and since updated and much enlarged as *The New Book of Middle Eastern Food*, is considered to be the cookery bible among Jews. She kindly gave me permission to feature any recipe from the book of my choosing, and given the many delights to pick from, narrowing down the choice was no straightforward task. In the end I went for her *ghormeh sabzi* because it celebrates my best-loved meat, lamb, with some amazing herbs and spices. It's no wonder that this dish was the favorite of Iranian Jews and remains one of the most popular dishes eaten in Iran today.

Lamb Ghormeh Sabzi

Serves 6

1/3 cup vegetable oil, divided

1 large onion, minced

2¼lb boneless lamb shoulder, excess fat trimmed, cut into 1-inch cubes

1 quart water

3 dried limes

1 teaspoon dried lime powder (or use an extra lime if you can't find it)

2 leeks, green parts included, trimmed, cleaned, and chopped

8 scallions, green parts included, chopped

1 large bunch of flat-leaf parsley, chopped

1 small bunch of cilantro, chopped

1 small bunch of dill, chopped

1 small bunch of fresh fenugreek leaves, chopped, or 2 tablespoons dried leaves

sea salt and freshly ground black pepper

Heat 2 tablespoons of the oil in a large, heavy saucepan, add the onion, and fry gently for around 10 minutes until soft. Add the lamb, turning the pieces over until they are nicely browned all over. Add the measured water and bring to a boil, skimming any scum that rises to the surface, then turn down the heat. Puncture the dried limes with the tip of a sharp knife and add them to the meat along with the dried lime powder. Season with salt and black pepper.

As soon as you have put the meat in, prepare the green vegetables and herbs. Add the chopped leeks and scallions to your food processor and pulse until they are very finely chopped.

Heat the remaining oil in a separate large saucepan, add the vegetables and herbs, and sauté over medium heat, stirring often, until they begin to darken. Add to the meat (if you are using dried fenugreek leaves, add these now too) and cook everything together over low heat, covered, for around 1½ to 2 hours until the meat is really tender. As the limes soften, squeeze them with the back of a spoon against the side of the pan so that they absorb the liquid and cease to float on the surface.

Serve over plain basmati rice.

Note

Dried limes and lime powder are available from Middle Eastern, Turkish, or Asian supermarkets.

Hamin (if you're Sephardi) or *cholent* (if you're Ashkenazi) is one of the only dishes that can actually be called truly Jewish. Jews adopted recipes from the countries in which they settled, often adapting them to kosher dietary laws, so they were in fact interpretations of existing dishes. Hamin is the exception, having been created specifically for Jews observing the rules of the Sabbath when cooking is prohibited. It was prepared on a Friday before the Sabbath started and then kept on a hot plate until after synagogue on the Saturday. This is an assembly job rather than real cooking, as you simply add everything to a slow cooker and leave for 12 to 15 hours. There is no need to tend the cooker; just let it work its magic. It won't be the most attractive dish you'll ever cook, but it's tasty enough that you can forgive its rather dull brown appearance.

"Hamin" Jewish Stew

Serves 6

2¼lb potatoes, peeled and halved, or leave whole if they are small

2 large onions, diced

2¼lb boneless lamb shoulder, excess fat trimmed, cut into 1-inch cubes

3 marrow bones

1 tablespoon sea salt

½ teaspoon freshly ground black pepper

¾ cup wheat grains or pearl barley, soaked in cold water for 8 hours

¾ cup dried chickpeas, soaked in cold water for 8 hours

6 eggs in their shells, well washed

3 garlic cloves, peeled but left whole

1 quart chicken stock

2 teaspoons sweet paprika

2 teaspoons ground turmeric

2 teaspoons ground cumin

Place the potatoes in the bottom of a 6- to 8½-quart slow cooker, then scatter them with the onions. Place the lamb and marrow bones on top and season everything with salt and pepper.

Drain and rinse the wheat or pearly barley and the chickpeas, then add to the cooker with the eggs and garlic cloves.

Heat the chicken stock and mix in the spices, then pour the mixture evenly over the contents of the slow cooker, topping off with water if necessary to ensure that everything is covered.

Cover the cooker pot, set it to low, and let cook for 12 to 15 hours.

To serve, shell the eggs and then pile the stew onto plates, adding an egg to each.

Tips

* You could use lamb on the bone instead, provided your slow cooker is big enough to accommodate it.

* If you don't own a slow cooker, use a large Dutch oven and ensure that there is enough water to cover the contents, then let cook in an oven preheated to 200°F overnight or for 12 to 14 hours.

I once cooked a lamb shank dish for my family when they came to visit me at my shared apartment in London. My kitchen was small and poorly equipped, and the oven and stove could be described at best as ropy. Wanting to impress, I spent a fortune on some beautiful shanks, which I lovingly marinated overnight, only to completely destroy them. The oven had packed up just an hour into the three-hour cooking process, so I transferred them to the stove and proceeded to boil them on too high a heat until they took on the texture of shoe leather. Watching my parents and sisters trying to cut (or rather saw) into them was painful to watch when the meat should have been falling off the bone. They teased me for a long time afterward whenever the words "lamb shanks" came up, which is why I was determined to redeem myself. Some 15 years later I decided to revisit the dish in preparation for the finals of *MasterChef* when I tried several different cooking techniques to hit optimum meat-melting consistency. Using the oven is definitely the best option to ensure that the temperature stays even, but I have also cooked this dish in the pressure cooker and it's a close second. So this recipe was born out of my quest for culinary lamb-shank redemption, and I can assure you that the meat will fall off the bone, bearing no resemblance to shoe leather.

Lamb Shank Tagine

Serves 4

2 teaspoons ras el hanout
sea salt
½ cup all-purpose flour
4 frenched lamb shanks
2 tablespoons olive oil, divided
1 onion, finely sliced
1 teaspoon ground cumin
1 teaspoon ground coriander
½ teaspoon ground cardamom
1 teaspoon ground sumac
1 teaspoon ground cinnamon
1 teaspoon dried lime powder
1 teaspoon smoked paprika
1 teaspoon ground turmeric
2 tablespoons tomato paste
1 large tomato, chopped
Continued...

Preheat the oven to 320°F.

Mix the ras el hanout and some salt into the flour, then roll the shanks in the seasoned flour until they are well coated.

Add 1 tablespoon of the oil to a large Dutch oven and brown the shanks all over; do this relatively slowly so that you get a nice caramelization on the lamb without burning the spice. Transfer the shanks to a plate and set them aside.

Heat the remaining oil in the Dutch oven over medium heat, add the onion, and fry until softened and lightly golden. Add the remaining flour mixture from the shanks to make a roux and fry for a couple of minutes until it is all incorporated. Add all the spices and stir well into the onion mixture, then add the tomato paste and fresh tomato.

Return the shanks to the Dutch oven, rolling them thoroughly in the onion and spices to coat. Then add the chicken stock (top off with water if the level of the liquid looks too low; you want the lamb to be almost covered) and add the thyme. Bring the liquid to a boil, cover with the lid, and place in the oven.

2 cups chicken stock

3 sprigs of thyme

6 black garlic cloves

2 teaspoons pomegranate molasses

10 dates, pitted

freshly ground black pepper

To garnish

¼ cup sliced almonds

3 ready-to-eat dried apricots,
thinly sliced

seeds from 1 pomegranate, or a small
tub of ready-prepared seeds

small handful of flat-leaf parsley,
finely chopped

Cook for 2 hours, then remove the lid and add the black garlic cloves, pomegranate molasses, and dates. Continue cooking for a further 30 minutes, by which time the sauce will have thickened slightly. If you would prefer to reduce it further, transfer the lamb shanks to a plate and bring the sauce to a simmer on the stove until it reaches the desired consistency.

Check for seasoning and add a touch of salt if needed and a few grindings of black pepper.

Heat a dry skillet over medium heat, add the sliced almonds, and toast, moving them around in the skillet, until lightly golden.

Transfer the lamb shanks and sauce to a large serving bowl and scatter with the apricots, pomegranate seeds, toasted almonds, and parsley.

Serve with couscous.

Stuffed cabbage leaves is the dish my mom recalls her mother making the most. Being Polish, it was one of the classics in her repertoire. In parts of Eastern Europe, it's traditional to serve these with a sour tomato and lemon sauce, but I've introduced a Sephardi-style *chraimeh* sauce to the story for an extra flavor dimension and a touch of heat. Some other little additional treats such as barberries and pistachios crept in there too for added texture.

Bubba Rose's Beef and Pistachio Stuffed Cabbage Leaves in Chraimeh Sauce "Holishkes"

Serves 4; makes around 10 to 12 rolls

1 large pointed cabbage
¼ cup Harissa (*see* page 17)

For the chraimeh sauce
3 tablespoons olive oil
3 red bell peppers
1 onion, coarsely diced
6 garlic cloves, sliced
2 red chiles, seeded and coarsely chopped
2 tablespoons smoked paprika
1 tablespoon ground cumin
1 teaspoon ground allspice
3 tablespoons tomato paste
14oz can good-quality diced tomatoes
2 cups chicken or vegetable stock
sea salt and freshly ground black pepper

For the stuffing
1lb 2oz ground beef
1 cup cooked basmati rice
2 tablespoons dried barberries
3 tablespoons coarsely chopped unsalted pistachio nuts
1 teaspoon sea salt
2 teaspoons Lebanese 7-spice Mix (*see* page 14)

Bring a large saucepan of water to a boil. Trim off the bottom of the cabbage, add whole to the boiling water and cook for 3 to 4 minutes until the leaves have softened and turned slightly transparent. Drain and refresh under cold running water to stop any further cooking, then set aside.

For the sauce, preheat the broiler to high. Rub a little of the olive oil all over each red bell pepper and season lightly with salt and black pepper. Place the peppers under the broiler for around 10 to 15 minutes, turning once, until the skins have blackened. Transfer to a resealable plastic food bag or bowl and immediately seal or cover with plastic wrap, then let stand for 20 minutes or so until cool enough to handle and the skins have loosened. Remove the skins with the back of a knife and discard the stalks and seeds, then coarsely chop the flesh.

Heat the remaining oil in a wide stove-to-oven dish, preferably with a lid. Add the onion, garlic, and chiles and sauté over medium heat for 10 minutes until the onions have started to soften. Stir in the spices and cook for a further 5 minutes before adding the bell peppers, tomato paste, canned tomatoes, and stock. Simmer the sauce, uncovered, for 30 minutes, then season with 1 teaspoon salt and black pepper to taste. Transfer the sauce to a blender and blitz until smooth. There is no need to wash the dish at this point, as you will be using it again. Set the sauce aside while you assemble the cabbage.

Add all the stuffing ingredients to a bowl and give everything a good stir.

Peel the outer leaves from the cooled cabbage, being careful not to break them, and lay them on a clean dish cloth or some paper towels to absorb some of the excess water. You can keep the leaves that are too small to stuff for serving with the dish. Using a small paring knife, carefully shave off some of the thick stalk at the base of each leaf, being careful not to cut through the leaf. Lay out a leaf in front of you with the stalk end closest to you. Add a teaspoon of the harissa and spread it over the leaf. Take about a tablespoonful of the stuffing, roll into a fat sausage shape, and place at

the base of the leaf. Fold the base of the leaf over the stuffing and then bring in the sides and roll up. The roll should be compact and the filling secure. Continue until you have used all the decent-sized leaves.

Spread a few tablespoonfuls of the sauce in the bottom of the stove-to-oven dish you used to cook it in. Place the cabbage rolls on top, packing them as tightly together as possible, then pour the remaining sauce over the rolls and bring everything up to a simmer. Cover the dish and cook very gently for an hour. It might be worth checking the liquid halfway through and if necessary add a small amount of boiling water.

When the cooking time is up, using tongs, transfer the stuffed cabbage leaves carefully to a serving plate and top with the sauce.

Tips

* You can prepare the stuffing mixture the day before to allow the flavors to develop and make it easier to roll.

* I would highly recommend making a double quantity of the sauce, as it's so versatile that you will want to keep a batch in the freezer.

I became obsessed with beef short ribs ever since eating them for the first time on a trip to New York a few years ago. I now order them whenever they appear on a menu and have spent as much time experimenting with how to cook them best as I have eating them. Short ribs are now widely available at most butchers or can be ordered in advance. Cook these ribs until the meat is clinging to the bones for dear life and have plenty of napkins at the ready; these are super sticky and lip-smackingly good.

Sticky Beef Short Ribs

Serves 6

1 tablespoon canola oil

8 beef short ribs, about 4½lb in total, trimmed of any large excess pieces of fat

2 large carrots, peeled and halved

2 celery stalks

2 onions, peeled but left whole

2 star anise

1 cinnamon stick

1½ quarts beef stock

1 tablespoon smoked paprika

3 tablespoons date syrup

1 tablespoon liquid honey

sea salt and freshly ground black pepper

Preheat the oven to 350°F.

Heat the oil in a wide, shallow skillet over high heat, and when it is almost smoking, sear the ribs until nicely browned.

Place the short ribs in an even layer in a deep roasting pan and season well with salt and pepper. Add the carrots, celery, onions, star anise, and cinnamon to the pan, then add the beef stock. Cover the pan with foil so it is sealed well and cook for 2½ to 3 hours until the meat is falling off the bone, turning the ribs over twice during the cooking process.

Remove the roasting pan from the oven, transfer the ribs to a shallow baking pan lined with foil (which means fewer dishes to wash later), and cover loosely with foil to keep them warm.

Strain the liquid into a saucepan and discard the vegetables and aromatics. Add the smoked paprika, date syrup, and honey and bring to a boil. Continue to boil over high heat for up to 30 minutes or until the mixture is reduced to a thick, syrupy consistency.

Preheat the broiler to high. Pour the sauce over each rib, using a basting brush to ensure that all sides are well coated, then flash under the broiler for 2 to 3 minutes until the tops are slightly caramelized.

Transfer the ribs to a plate and serve immediately.

Tip

When I make these for the kids, I shred the meat and serve with the sauce over macaroni or Spaetzle (see page 108).

My Aunty Rachel kindly spent one of her precious vacation days when she came over on a visit from Israel cooking with me in my kitchen, and from that I inherited two wonderful dishes, this one and the Hot Red Bell Pepper Fish Stew (*see* page 123). Stuffed artichokes are very popular in Morocco where Rachel's family came from, and there is such a lovely contrast of flavors here in the warm-spiced ground beef and the slightly sharp taste of the artichokes. Most Middle Eastern or Turkish supermarkets stock artichoke bottoms in a jar, but if you can't get those, feel free to use frozen ones, which are widely available, or of course fresh ones when they are in season. Serve with Israeli "Chik Chak" Salad (*see* page 172).

Aunty Rachel's Beef-stuffed Artichokes

Serves 4

juice of ½ lemon (if using fresh artichokes)

8 artichoke bottoms from a jar, or use frozen if you prefer or fresh when available

2 large eggs

1¼ cups all-purpose flour, seasoned with sea salt and freshly ground pepper

¼ cup olive oil

For the stuffing

1 small onion, finely diced

9oz ground beef

2 teaspoons ground cumin

2 teaspoons baharat

2 teaspoons sweet paprika

½ teaspoon sea salt

½ teaspoon freshly ground black pepper

2 large handfuls of flat-leaf parsley, finely chopped

For the sauce

1 tablespoon mushroom or chicken stock powder

½ teaspoon freshly ground black pepper

2 cups hot water

Mix all the ingredients for the stuffing together in a bowl, reserving 1 tablespoon of the parsley for garnish. If using fresh artichoke bottoms, rub them with the lemon juice. Stuff each artichoke with 2 tablespoons of the filling, pressing it down well to make it nice and compact.

Beat the eggs in a shallow bowl, and spread the seasoned flour out on a plate. Carefully roll the stuffed artichokes in the beaten egg, then coat in the seasoned flour, dusting off any excess.

Heat the olive oil in a wide, heavy skillet large enough to hold the artichokes in a single layer. When it is hot but not smoking, add the artichokes (in batches if necessary), meat-side down, and fry over medium heat for 3 to 4 minutes until the meat is nicely browned on top. Turn them over and fry for a further 3 minutes.

To make the sauce, mix the stock powder and black pepper into the measured hot water until well combined. Put all the artichokes back into the pan, if necessary, and pour in the stock. Simmer, uncovered, for 20 minutes, basting the top of the artichokes every so often, until the sauce has reduced slightly and the artichokes are tender.

Serve the stuffed artichokes immediately, drizzled with some of the sauce and garnished with the reserved parsley.

Tip

The ground beef stuffing can be used for so many other dishes: meatballs, burgers, as a variation on a cottage pie, or formed into koftas. I've given quantities to make enough stuffing to fill the number of artichoke bottoms specified, but feel free to double the amounts and use it for another dish, as suggested.

Some very fond childhood memories stir when I say these two words: salt beef. Trips to Selfridges' salt beef bar were the ultimate reward, a treat to mark some sort of special occasion. I also remember sitting in a diner in New York, Sammy's, that my parents had talked about many a time, where the salt beef on rye sandwich was far taller than the length of my jaw and the pickles were wickedly sharp and crunchy. I had never even thought about making it myself. Rather like filo pastry, why would you make something that's much easier and just as tasty to buy? Well, in the here and now, I am making it myself, and yes, it's a process, and yes, you need to decide that you want to cook it at least a week before you plan to serve it, but it is so unbelievably satisfying, loads more economical, and I don't mind admitting how much I love the praise that gets heaped on me when I serve it with a slightly smug smile.

Salt Beef

Serves around 12 with some left over for later

For the brine
1⅓ cups coarse sea salt
1½ soft light brown sugar
2 teaspoons allspice berries
2 teaspoons juniper berries
2 teaspoons coriander seeds
2 teaspoons black peppercorns
1½oz Prague powder #1
4 bay leaves
3 cloves
4 quarts cold water

For the brisket
6½lb piece of flat brisket, fatty if possible
½ garlic bulb, unpeeled
2 celery stalks
1 onion, peeled but left whole
2 carrots, peeled but left whole
3 bay leaves
handful of herbs, such as flat leaf parsley and thyme, or 1 bouquet garni

To serve
mustard
gherkins

Add all the brine seasonings to a very large saucepan and cover with the measured cold water. Bring to a boil and immediately turn off the heat, then let cool completely.

When the brine is cool, transfer it, along with the brisket, to a very large nonmetallic container with a lid. Find a weight of some sort to keep the meat submerged in the liquid—a bottle or heavy plate should do the trick—add the lid, and then preferably place in the fridge if you can find enough space, or alternatively somewhere else pretty cold. If making in the winter, leaving the container outside would work, provided that it is well sealed. The meat needs to be left to brine for at least 7 days and up to 10, turning it over in the liquid once each day.

When you are ready to cook, rinse the brisket really well in cold water. Roll the brisket into a cylinder shape and tie with kitchen string to secure. Place it in a large saucepan with the remaining brisket ingredients, cover with cold water, and bring to a very light simmer. Cover with the lid and let simmer very gently for around 2 to 3 hours or until a skewer goes in effortlessly.

Let the brisket cool slightly in the water, then lift the lovely wobbly hunk of meat out. Carve the meat into thick generous slices and serve it with mustard and gherkins.

The salt beef will keep for up to a week in the fridge and reheat really well, but just make sure that it's properly sealed in an airtight container.

Note

The Prague powder #1 is integral to achieving that lovely pink color inside, so please don't omit it; it's available online.

My mom's classic oxtail stew is comfort food at its best and the dish that evokes the greatest amount of nostalgia. It will benefit from being made a day or two ahead of serving, as the flavors deeply intensify the longer they are left to sit. If there are no slurping noises as you suck the juices and goodness from the bones and no licking of fingers around the table as you eat these, then you are most definitely not eating them correctly. *Spaetzle*, pronounced "shpetzley," are soft egg noodles widely eaten across parts of Northern and Eastern Europe, and are named after their "little sparrow"-like appearance. My Polish grandmother would make these frequently. I would highly advise investing in a spaetzle maker (inexpensive and easily available online), because you too will want to make these regularly.

Oxtail Stew with Spaetzle

Serves 8

⅓ cup all-purpose flour

4½lb beef oxtail pieces

3 tablespoons vegetable oil, plus extra if needed

3 large carrots, peeled and cut into chunks

3 celery stalks, chopped

2 onions, diced

1 turnip, peeled and cut into chunks

3 tablespoons tomato paste

2 cups beef stock

bottle of red wine

1 bouquet garni

3 bay leaves

sea salt and freshly ground black pepper

For the spaetzle

3 eggs

1½ cups milk

4 cups all-purpose flour

½ teaspoon table salt

2 tablespoons butter

sea salt (if needed) and freshly ground black pepper

Preheat the oven to 300°F.

Spread the flour on a plate, season generously with salt and black pepper, and roll the oxtail pieces in the seasoned flour to coat.

Heat the oil in a large Dutch oven and fry the oxtail pieces quickly in batches over high heat to color; don't overcrowd the pan. Transfer with a slotted spoon to a plate, keeping some of the juices in the pan.

Add more oil to the pan if needed and then the vegetables. Sauté for a few minutes until they start to soften slightly and take on some color. Stir in the tomato paste and cook for 2 minutes, then return the oxtail to the pan, cover with the stock and red wine, and add the bouquet garni and bay leaves. If the liquid doesn't quite cover the meat, top off with a little more water. Bring to a simmer, then cover with the lid and place in the oven for around 4 to 5 hours, stirring every hour or so and making sure there is enough liquid, until the meat is falling off the bone and the sauce is nice and rich.

About 20 minutes before you are ready to serve, bring a saucepan of water to a boil. Make the spaetzle dough by beating the eggs in a large bowl for a few seconds until bubbly. Add the milk and beat to combine. Sift the flour and salt on the top and fold in. The batter will be thick and very elastic but should be loose, so if you need to, add a little more water.

If you don't have a spaetzle maker, add the batter to a pastry bag and make a small opening at the end, then squeeze small pieces of the batter out over the pan of boiling water. Alternatively, add the batter to your spaetzle maker and cook following the manufacturers' directions. The spaetzle are ready when they have floated to the surface of the water and are nice and fluffy; this will take no more than 2 to 3 minutes. Transfer to a bowl with a slotted spoon and repeat until you have used up all the batter. Add the butter, some black pepper and sea salt if needed, and mix together.

To serve, divide the spaetzle among plates and top with the oxtail stew.

This dish is a real showstopper and it managed to unanimously unite the guest judges on *MasterChef*, Ping, Luke, and Jack (winner and finalists on *MasterChef* 2014), when I cooked it for them. The chickpeas and the Moroccan pesto, better known in North Africa and the Middle East as *chermoula*, have very powerful flavors, but somehow manage to complement rather than overpower the soft and delicate nature of the sea bass. I would normally advocate always using freshly cooked chickpeas, but with the time constraints of the TV program, I had no choice but to use canned and I think they work just as well in this dish, plus they strip out one extra process.

I practiced this dish on family and friends so many times. I think my husband and I must have eaten no fewer than 15 versions of it, but I still love it just as much, especially served with a nice cold glass of Riesling.

Sea Bass over Spiced Chickpeas with Confit Cherry Tomatoes and Moroccan Pesto

Serves 4

4 sea bass fillets
sea salt and freshly ground black pepper
olive oil, for shallow-frying

For the chickpeas
1 cup dried chickpeas, soaked in cold water overnight, or 2 × 14oz cans chickpeas
2 teaspoons ground coriander
2 teaspoons ground cumin
1 teaspoon caraway seeds
2 teaspoons ground sumac
1 teaspoon freshly ground black pepper
2 teaspoons sweet smoked paprika
½ teaspoon cayenne pepper, or to taste
½ teaspoon sea salt
½ cup olive oil
2 garlic cloves, minced
1 tablespoon chopped rosemary leaves
sea salt, if needed

For the Moroccan pesto
6 large handfuls of cilantro
Continued...

For the chickpeas, if using dried, drain them of their soaking water, rinse, and place in a large saucepan. Cover with plenty of fresh cold water and bring to a boil. Cook for around an hour until soft, then drain and let steam-dry. If using canned, drain and rinse them really well, then set aside.

To make the pesto, coarsely chop the cilantro, preserved lemon skins, garlic, ginger, and chiles and add to a food processor along with the cumin and some salt. Pulse a few times until everything is very finely chopped. Then with the motor running, drizzle the olive oil in slowly until you have a loose consistency like pesto. Transfer to a bowl, cover, and let stand in the fridge while you prepare the rest of the dish, to allow the flavors to develop.

For the confit tomatoes, preheat the oven to 250°F. Put the tomatoes on a baking pan lined with foil, add all the other confit ingredients, and toss together, ensuring that the tomatoes are well coated with the oil and seasonings. Roast for around 1½ hours or until the tomatoes have slightly dehydrated. Remove from the oven and set aside.

Mix all the spices and salt for the chickpeas together. Heat the oil gently in a deep saucepan large enough to hold the chickpeas and when the oil is warm (you don't want it hot, otherwise the spices and garlic will burn), add the mixed spices, garlic, and rosemary and stir together for a couple of minutes. Then add the chickpeas and cook until everything is nice and hot. Check for seasoning, as this is a good time to add extra cayenne for more of a kick. Remove from the heat and cover with a lid or some foil while you cook the fish.

4 preserved lemons, halved, flesh scooped out and discarded

4 garlic cloves, peeled

1½-inch piece of fresh ginger root, peeled

3 large green chiles, seeded

1 teaspoon ground cumin

sea salt

⅓ to ½ cup olive oil, divided

For the confit cherry tomatoes

12 cherry tomatoes, halved

1 tablespoon olive oil

1 teaspoon sea salt

1 teaspoon granulated sugar

1 garlic clove, crushed

freshly ground black pepper

Run your fingers down the flesh side of the sea bass fillets to make sure that all the bones have been removed (a pair of tweezers are handy for removing them if necessary), and if desired, trim the bottom and top of the fillets on the diagonal to make for a neater presentation. Season the sea bass fillets on both sides with salt and black pepper. Heat a large skillet, or 2 if you can't fit the fish into one, over high heat and add a tablespoon of olive oil. When it is smoking, add the fish, skin-side down, and press down gently on the flesh with a spatula to stop it from curling. Be careful at this point, as the oil will spatter a bit. Turn the heat down very slightly and let the fish cook, undisturbed, for 3 minutes. You can tell when the fish is almost done by checking the translucency. Turn the fish over carefully and cook on the other side for 1 minute, or a maximum of 2 minutes if they are particularly large fillets.

Transfer the fish, flesh-side down, to a plate to rest while you assemble the rest of the dish.

Give the pesto a stir and add a bit more olive oil if needed. Place a few heaped tablespoonfuls of the chickpeas on the plate, 6 cherry tomato halves around the chickpeas, and then top with the sea bass, skin-side up, adding a line of pesto over the fish and a drizzle around the plate.

Tip

I prefer to use whole spices where possible for the chickpea seasoning. Toast the coriander and cumin seeds in large quantities in a dry skillet over medium heat until fragrant, shaking the pan constantly, then grind them with a spice grinder or power blender so that you always have this mixture on hand. It's great with other legumes such as cannellini and cranberry beans, or a lovely addition for enhancing a basic tomato sauce.

I have loved using dukkah ever since I discovered it on my travels in Egypt. I use it like a pesto on almost anything, and when I first tried it on a simple piece of white fish, I knew it was a recipe I had to share. The crunch against the soft white flesh of the fish gives a lovely texture combination and it's one of those dishes that requires very little effort for an impressive result. Feel free to substitute any other meaty white fish such as hake or halibut for the cod; it even works well with salmon. The dish needs few accompaniments other than some buttered green beans or a fresh green salad.

Cod Loin with a Dukkah Crust

Serves 4

4 cod loins
½ teaspoon sea salt
freshly ground black pepper

For the crust
1 quantity Dukkah (*see* page 16)
2 tablespoons olive oil

Preheat the oven to 350°F.

For the crust, add the dukkah to a shallow bowl and slowly drizzle in the olive oil until the mixture is nice and moist.

Place the cod loins on a baking pan, season with the salt and some black pepper, and spread the crust mixture evenly and generously over the top of each piece.

Bake for 10 to 12 minutes, depending on the thickness of the loins, until the crust is golden and the fish is cooked through.

My dad used to make this a lot for us; it was one of the few dishes he could make by himself. Its simplicity is what makes it so special—maximum flavor from minimal effort. The sesame oil and almonds work so well together with the earthiness of the trout. I would recommend removing the heads of the fish before serving to anyone who may have a squeamish disposition.

Pan-fried Trout with Sesame and Almonds

Serves 2

1 tablespoon olive oil
2 whole trout, gutted and scaled
1 tablespoon toasted sesame oil
½ cup sliced almonds
sea salt and freshly ground black pepper

To serve
buttered new potatoes
green beans
crisp green salad

Start by heating the olive oil in a large skillet over medium-high heat until nice and hot.

Season the trout with salt and black pepper and add to the skillet. Turn the heat down to medium and fry for 5 minutes on one side.

Turn the fish over and add the sesame oil and sliced almonds, then cook for a further 5 minutes.

Serve immediately with buttered new potatoes and green beans or a crisp green salad.

This salmon recipe is so easy and is equally good served hot with plain boiled rice and green beans, or at room temperature with my Buckwheat and Barberry Salad (*see* page 188). It takes very little time to prepare, and dotted with some little pomegranate gems, it looks delightful on the plate. You can also serve this to kids; the sweetness of the pomegranate is an instant winner.

Sticky Pomegranate Salmon

Serves 4

2 teaspoons soft dark brown sugar

1 teaspoon ground sumac

1 teaspoon cornstarch

½ teaspoon sea salt

4 skin-on salmon fillets

freshly ground black pepper

1 tablespoon vegetable or peanut oil

1 tablespoon pomegranate molasses

Buckwheat and Barberry Salad with Spiced Pomegranate Dressing (*see* page 188), to serve

seeds from ½ pomegranate, to garnish

Preheat the oven to 400°F.

Mix the sugar, sumac, cornstarch, and salt together, then rub over the flesh side of the salmon fillets and add a grinding of black pepper over the top.

Heat an ovenproof skillet over high heat and add the oil. When it is very hot, add the salmon fillets, flesh-side down, and reduce the heat to medium. Sear for 2 minutes, then turn the fillets over and cook on the skin side for a further minute. Using a pastry brush, spread the pomegranate molasses evenly over each fillet.

Transfer the pan to the oven and cook for a further 8 to 10 minutes.

If you don't have an ovenproof skillet, transfer the salmon to a baking pan lined with foil before placing in the oven.

Serve the salmon at room temperature on a bed of buckwheat and barberry salad and garnished with pomegranate seeds.

I like to involve my kids in the preparation of these, as their little hands make surprisingly neat little cakes. This works really well as an appetizer served on a bed of the Fennel, Orange, and Carrot Salad (*see* page 187) or as a lovely family dinner. The fishcakes benefit from being made a little in advance and chilled so that they hold together better when fried.

Salmon and Sweet Potato Fishcakes with Lime Za'atar Yogurt

Serves 4 as a main or 6 as an appetizer; makes around 14 fishcakes

3 tablespoons olive oil, divided
2 sweet potatoes, around 1lb 2oz in total, scrubbed
4 skinless salmon fillets (or remove skin), about 1½lb in total
1 small bunch of dill
8 black peppercorns
1 small bunch of cilantro leaves, finely chopped
juice of 1 lemon
3 tablespoons all-purpose flour
2 eggs, beaten
2¼ cups medium matzo meal
sea salt and freshly ground black pepper

For the lime za'atar yogurt
2 cups plain yogurt
1 tablespoon Za'atar (*see* page 15)
grated zest and juice of 2 limes

Preheat the oven to 400°F.

Rub 1 tablespoon of the oil into the sweet potatoes and season with salt and black pepper, then place them on a baking pan and roast for about 40 minutes to 1 hour, depending on their size, until cooked all the way through. Let cool while you make the fishcakes.

Place the salmon fillets in a wide, shallow pan with the dill and peppercorns, and barely cover with water. Gently poach, uncovered, for 8 to 10 minutes until just cooked through. Lift the salmon from the poaching liquid and flake into a large bowl.

Halve the sweet potatoes, scoop out the flesh, and add to the fish along with the cilantro and lemon juice. Season well with salt and black pepper and mix together thoroughly. If you have the time, cover and chill the mixture in the fridge for 30 minutes to make the cakes easier to form. Shape the mixture into palm-sized cakes.

Put the flour, eggs, and matzo meal in 3 separate shallow bowls. Season the flour with salt and black pepper, then coat the cakes in the seasoned flour, dip into the beaten egg, and then roll in the matzo meal. Repeat the egg and matzo meal coating for a second time if you want an extra-crispy fishcake.

Place the fishcakes on a tray lined with nonstick parchment paper or foil and refrigerate until you are ready to fry.

Mix the ingredients for the lime za'atar yogurt together in a bowl, then cover and refrigerate until you are ready to serve.

Heat the remaining 2 tablespoons of oil in a wide skillet and fry the fishcakes, in batches, over medium heat for around 3 minutes on each side until they are nicely golden.

Serve with a generous spoonful of the yogurt on the side and a crisp salad.

Tip

If you can't find matzo meal, you can substitute any other bread crumbs of your choice; panko would be my next favorite.

I made a version of this recipe on *MasterChef* to achieve a place in the final line-up of three contestants. The guest judge happened to be the guru of fish, Nathan Outlaw, and the dish was very much given the thumbs-up. I served it with spiced meat-stuffed Turkish manti (like tiny ravioli) and some fancy garnishes, but it was the sauce that was the star of the show and overshadowed all the other elements on the plate. I have pared my recipe back to make cooking this special occasion dish much simpler and used meaty monkfish, which stands up well to the robust flavors in the sauce.

Moroccan Spiced Monkfish with Fennel, Leek, and Cream Sauce

Serves 4

2 tablespoons olive oil, divided

3 teaspoons ras el hanout, divided

2 thick pieces of monkish fillet, around ¾lb each

1 large fennel bulb, woody stalk and core removed and fronds reserved to garnish, very thinly sliced (preferably with a mandoline if you have one)

1 large leek, white part only, trimmed, cleaned, and finely diced

2 garlic cloves, minced

½ teaspoon ground turmeric

2 tablespoons white wine

2 cups vegetable stock

1 cup heavy cream

1 heaped teaspoon Dijon mustard

½ teaspoon sea salt

freshly ground black pepper

To serve
steamed green beans, drizzled with oil and lemon juice
buttered steamed new potatoes

Mix 1 tablespoon of the oil with 1 heaped teaspoon of the ras el hanout in a small bowl to make a loose paste. Spread over the monkfish fillets in a dish using a pastry brush, cover and let marinate in the fridge for an hour.

Preheat the oven to 400°F.

Heat the remaining tablespoon of oil in a large, deep skillet over high heat, and when it is smoking, add the monkfish and sear quickly until it is golden brown on all sides.

Transfer the monkfish to a baking pan and roast for 10 to 12 minutes until it is cooked through. Remove from the oven and let rest for a few minutes under some tented foil.

While the monkfish is roasting, add to the same skillet you used to sear the fish the fennel, leek, garlic, remaining ras el hanout, and turmeric. Stir together for a couple of minutes before deglazing the pan with the white wine. Let the wine cook out for a minute, stirring constantly, then add the stock. Turn the heat down very slightly and let the sauce bubble away and reduce for 10 minutes or until its reduced by two-thirds. Add the cream and the mustard and keep stirring for a further 3 minutes. Season with the salt and black pepper to taste.

Divide the sauce between 4 shallow bowls or plates. Slice the monkish into generous pieces and place neatly on top of the sauce in the center. Serve immediately, scattered with the reserved fennel fronds, with some green beans drizzled with oil and lemon juice, and a bowl of buttered new potatoes on the side.

I am so lucky to have married into an extended family of outstanding cooks. My husband's Aunty Rachel is one of those women who makes cooking look effortless. She glides around her kitchen in Israel, and more recently my kitchen when she came to help, working so fast that I couldn't keep up with my pen and pad. I kept handing her spoons in the hope that she would at least give me some calculated measurements, but her instinct, like many confident cooks, was just to throw in a pinch of this and a drizzle of that, working only by sight and taste. I have constructed this recipe as best I can, but would ask with this one, like many others of mine, that you use your own judgment when it comes to the spicy seasoning. It has some heat, yet not enough to detract from the delicate fish. But feel free to be more heavy-handed with the Aleppo pepper if you prefer, or if you are substituting hot paprika for the Aleppo pepper, try adding a pinch of cayenne pepper, too.

Hot Red Bell Pepper Fish Stew

Serves 4

1 large red bell pepper, cored, seeded, and cut into thin rings

2 large ripe tomatoes, cut into medium-thick slices

1 green chile, seeds included, coarsely diced

⅓ cup canola oil

1 teaspoon sea salt, divided

½ teaspoon freshly ground black pepper

1 tablespoon Aleppo pepper or pul biber/Turkish red pepper flakes (or substitute hot paprika if you can't find either)

2 teaspoons sweet smoked paprika

½ cup water

4 skinless haddock or cod loins, around 5½oz each

juice of ½ lemon

2 large handfuls of cilantro leaves, coarsely chopped

3 garlic cloves, finely sliced

boiled rice or crusty bread, to serve

Lay the bell pepper rings in the bottom of a wide, shallow, ovenproof saucepan, then layer the tomatoes on top. Scatter with the diced chile.

Mix the oil, half the salt, the black pepper, Aleppo pepper, and paprika together. Pour the mixture over the vegetables, then top off with the measured water and bring to a simmer. Cover with a lid and cook over low heat for 30 minutes.

Set the fish pieces on top of the vegetables, squeeze over the lemon juice, and sprinkle with the remaining ½ teaspoon of salt, then scatter with the cilantro and garlic. Replace the lid and let simmer for a further 15 minutes, basting the fish with the liquid every few minutes.

Meanwhile, preheat the oven to 375°F.

Remove the lid from the pan and transfer it to the oven to cook for a further 20 minutes.

Serve with simple boiled rice or some crusty bread.

Big plates with vegetables

Freekeh, the ancient origins of which lie in the Middle East and North African regions, is made from green, unripe wheat and has become known as an alternative grain to couscous and rice. Its robust and nutty flavor lends itself perfectly to a risotto where it can stand up really well to strong spices. I cooked a freekeh risotto similar to this one on *MasterChef*, which I served with chicken and zucchini, but I have promoted it to centerstage here, as it needs little else in the way of accompaniments.

Freekeh Risotto with Roasted Cashews and Minted Sour Cream

Serves 4

2 tablespoons olive or canola oil

1 onion, minced

3 garlic cloves, minced

1 teaspoon ground cinnamon

1 teaspoon ground allspice

2 teaspoons ras el hanout

1½ cups freekeh, rinsed

2 cups vegetable or chicken stock, plus extra if needed

2/3 cup raw cashews

grated zest of 1 lemon

large handful of flat-leaf parsley, finely chopped, divided

1½ cups grated Parmesan cheese, divided

For the minted sour cream

1¼ cups sour cream

2 garlic cloves, crushed

1 tablespoon finely chopped mint

juice of ½ lemon, or to taste

sea salt and freshly ground black pepper

Heat the oil in a medium saucepan, add the onion and garlic, and gently sauté for around 10 minutes until softened. Add the spices and cook, stirring, for a couple of minutes, then add the freekeh and stock.

Cook, uncovered, over low heat for around 30 to 40 minutes until the freekeh is cooked through but still has a little bite. You may need to add a bit more stock if the liquid has been absorbed before the freekeh is ready.

Meanwhile, preheat the oven to 400°F. Spread the cashews out on a baking pan and roast for 10 minutes until golden. Let cool, then coarsely chop; you want them left as large as possible.

Once the freekeh is cooked, remove the pan from the heat and stir in the lemon zest along with all but a handful of the cashews, parsley, and Parmesan.

Mix all the ingredients for the minted sour cream together in a bowl and season to taste with salt and black pepper.

Ladle the risotto into shallow bowls, then scatter with the reserved cashews, parsley, and Parmesan. Top with some of the minted sour cream and serve.

Tip

Any leftover risotto can be shaped into little walnut-sized balls with dampened hands, then rolled in seasoned flour, beaten egg, and panko bread crumbs and deep-fried until golden brown.

I acquired this recipe some years ago after extracting it from a hotel chef in Cyprus. This style of couscous is typical across the Mediterranean, with so much flavor from so few ingredients, and works beautifully with my Chicken Shawarma with Jerusalem and Lebanese Spices (*see* page 76) or Cod Loin with a Dukkah Crust (*see* page 113). My kids are very happy with a bowl of this and nothing more than some grated cheese on top. I've kept the butter optional, as it's not strictly necessary, but it does add a lovely creamy flavor.

Mediterranean Couscous

Serves 4

2 tablespoons olive oil
1 small onion, chopped
⅓ cup broken dried vermicelli noodles
14oz can diced tomatoes
1 vegetable stock cube
1 cup coarse bulgur wheat
2 tablespoons unsalted butter (optional)
sea salt and freshly ground black pepper

Heat the olive oil in a medium saucepan, add the onion, and fry over medium heat until soft. Add the vermicelli and cook, stirring, with the onion until lightly golden.

Pour the canned tomatoes into the pan, then add the stock cube to the empty tomato can, pour in boiling water to fill the can about halfway, and stir to dissolve the cube.

Add the stock to the saucepan, bring the contents of the pan up to a boil, and add the bulgur wheat. Give it all a good stir to ensure that the bulgur is well incorporated into the tomatoes and then add the butter, if using.

Switch off the heat, cover the pan with a lid, and let the mixture stand for 20 to 25 minutes until the bulgur has cooked through. If it needs a little longer, just put the lid back on so that it can continue to steam. Once ready, fork through the grains and season generously with salt and black pepper.

Risotto is the ultimate comfort food. In my quest to find ways of simplifying the process while extracting the most flavor, this fragrant and creamy dish was born and it now features regularly at my supper clubs as a popular vegetarian main dish. Only the occasional stir is required; far lower maintenance than a traditional risotto and less cooking time, too.

Preserved Lemon Orzo and Butternut Squash Risotto with Sugar Snap Peas

Serves 6

3 tablespoons olive oil, divided

1 small white onion, minced

2 garlic cloves, minced

1 small butternut squash, peeled, seeded, and grated

1 cup orzo pasta

2¾ cups vegetable stock

2 small preserved lemons or 1 large, halved and seeds removed

3 tablespoons butter

½ cup grated Parmesan cheese

¼lb sugar snap peas

1 teaspoon fresh lemon juice

1 teaspoon ground sumac

sea salt and freshly ground black pepper

Heat 2 tablespoons of the oil in a saucepan, add the onion, and cook gently for 5 minutes, then add the garlic and continue cooking until the onion is soft and translucent. Add the butternut squash and cook for 5 minutes, then add the orzo, stirring well to incorporate.

Pour in the stock, turn the heat down to a simmer, and cover with a lid. Cook gently for around 10 to 15 minutes, stirring every so often so that the pasta doesn't stick.

While the risotto is cooking, blitz the preserved lemons in a blender, skin and all, to a paste and set aside.

The risotto is cooked when the orzo is nice and soft. Turn off the heat and add the preserved lemon paste, butter, and Parmesan, and season well with salt and black pepper. Give it all a good stir through and then leave the lid on while you prepare the sugar snap peas.

Heat the remaining tablespoon of oil in a wok over high heat, and when it is smoking, throw in the sugar snaps and stand back, as they will spatter and spit. Toss them in the wok for around a minute or so until they have charred slightly; you don't want to overcook them, as they should still be crunchy. Add a pinch of salt, the lemon juice, and sumac and give the pan a final shake.

Spoon a generous amount of risotto into shallow soup bowls or plates and then top with the sugar snaps and a final grinding of black pepper.

Tip

For fussy kids, just omit the preserved lemon paste, as it has quite a distinctive flavor that they may find a bit overpowering.

This dish makes a lovely and robust vegetarian main course. The warm spice from the ras el hanout paired with the braised fennel and soft chickpeas is a pleasing combination, and while there are a few processes involved to achieve the end result, it can all be prepared ahead and served at room temperature.

Moroccan Stuffed Sweet Potato with Braised Fennel and Tahini

Serves 4

2 large or 3 medium sweet potatoes, scrubbed

2 tablespoons olive oil, divided

sea salt

green salad or Israeli "Chik Chak" Salad (*see* page 172), to serve

For the stuffing

2 fennel bulbs

½ stick butter

1 cup vegetable or chicken stock

¼ cup mung beans, soaked in cold water overnight

1 onion, finely diced

2 fat garlic cloves, minced

14oz can chickpeas

1 teaspoon ras el hanout

½ teaspoon sea salt

2 large handfuls of cilantro, finely chopped

For the spiced date dressing

3 tablespoons extra virgin olive oil

1 tablespoon date syrup

2 teaspoons white balsamic vinegar

1 teaspoon ras el hanout

pinch of sea salt

freshly ground black pepper

For the tahini dressing

3 tablespoons tahini

1 tablespoon plain yogurt

juice of ½ lemon

pinch of sea salt

Preheat the oven to 400°F.

Cut the sweet potatoes in half lengthwise and place, cut-side down, on a baking pan. Rub a little of the olive oil over the skins and sprinkle lightly with sea salt. Bake in the oven for 40 to 45 minutes until tender.

For the stuffing, cut the woody stalks off the fennel bulbs, then cut the bulbs in half lengthwise. Melt the butter in a skillet over medium-high heat, and when it starts to foam, add the fennel, cut-side down. Reduce the heat to medium and cook the fennel for 15 minutes, turning every so often until both sides are golden. When the fennel has started to caramelize, add the stock and bring to a boil. Cover and cook for a further 5 minutes. Uncover and continue to cook for another 5 minutes until the stock has almost evaporated and the fennel is nearly cooked through but still retains some bite.

Drain and rinse the mung beans, then put in a saucepan and cover with plenty of cold water. Bring to a boil and boil for around 15 minutes until the beans are cooked through but not soft.

Meanwhile, heat the remaining olive oil in a pan, add the onion, and gently fry for 10 minutes until soft. Add the garlic and cook for a further 5 minutes. Drain and rinse the chickpeas, then add to the pan with the ras el hanout and salt. Cook until the chickpeas are coated in the spiced onions and warmed through. Drain the mung beans, then stir into the chickpea mixture and continue to cook for a couple of minutes. Transfer to a large bowl. Chop the braised fennel into bite-sized pieces and add to the bowl.

Whisk the ingredients for the spiced date dressing together in a small bowl.

In a separate bowl, mix the ingredients for the tahini dressing together, then add a little cold water while stirring until you achieve a pouring consistency.

To assemble, pour the spiced date dressing over the stuffing mixture, then add the cilantro and stir through. Transfer each sweet potato half to a plate, flesh-side up and make a deep cut down the center to create a hole for the stuffing. Spoon a generous amount of the stuffing into each potato half, then drizzle liberally with the tahini dressing. Serve the dish with any remaining tahini in a bowl on the side and accompanied by a green salad or Israeli "Chik Chak" Salad.

Eggplants are so meaty and their spongelike flesh makes them a great vegetable to stuff. There is texture to this dish as well as great flavor, and it can also be made ahead of time; just add the crumb before reheating and serving.

Tomato-stuffed Eggplant with a Sourdough and Walnut Crumb

Serves 4

2 large eggplants
1 teaspoon table salt
2 slices of sourdough bread
⅓ cup olive oil, divided
2 teaspoons Za'atar (*see* page 15)
½ cup walnut halves
1 tablespoon fresh thyme leaves
or 1 teaspoon dried thyme
1 large red onion, thinly sliced
1 teaspoon red wine vinegar
2 teaspoons soft dark brown sugar
3 garlic cloves, minced
1 teaspoon ground cumin
½ teaspoon ground cinnamon
1 teaspoon sweet paprika
14oz can diced tomatoes
½ teaspoon granulated sugar
1 cup vegetable stock
sea salt and freshly ground black pepper
a few fresh oregano leaves or a pinch
of dried oregano, to garnish (optional)

Preheat the oven to 350°F.

Halve the eggplants lengthwise and carefully scoop out the flesh, making sure that you leave approximately a ¹⁄₁₆-inch layer of flesh in the skins. Reserve the scooped-out flesh in a bowl for using later. Lightly sprinkle the eggplant skins with table salt and let stand in the fridge for 30 minutes.

Coarsely cube the sourdough and then toss with 1 tablespoon of the olive oil and the za'atar. Spread out on a baking pan and bake for 20 minutes until they have fully dried out. Add the walnuts to the pan and bake together for a further 10 minutes.

Transfer the sourdough and walnuts to a food processor, add the thyme, and pulse until the bread and nuts are a coarse rubble consistency.

Start the sauce by adding 2 tablespoons of the olive oil to a saucepan and frying the eggplant flesh over high heat until golden. Remove from the pan and set aside. Place the same pan back on the stove and reduce the heat to low. Add another tablespoon of oil and gently fry the onion until it is soft and translucent, then add the vinegar and brown sugar and cook, stirring, for a further 5 minutes until the onion starts to caramelize slightly. Add the garlic and spices and cook for 2 minutes before adding the canned tomatoes, eggplant flesh, granulated sugar, and sea salt to taste. Simmer gently, uncovered, for 10 minutes.

While the sauce is simmering, rinse the salt from the eggplant skins and pat dry gently with a dish cloth. Add the remaining tablespoon of oil to a skillet and fry the skins over medium heat for 5 minutes on each side (make sure you are wearing an apron for this stage, as they are likely to spatter and spit).

Transfer the eggplants to a deep-sided ovenproof dish or roasting pan; you want them to fit snugly side by side. Check the seasoning of the tomato sauce, then spoon generously into the skins. Grind some black pepper over the top and pour the stock into the pan around the eggplants. Cover with foil and bake for 20 minutes, then remove the foil, add the sourdough crumb, and bake for a further 10 minutes.

Serve with a garnish of fresh oregano leaves or a pinch of dried, if liked.

Amba is a spice commonly used throughout Israel. It has a tangy, sharp, and slightly spicy flavor that can really enhance a humble everyday vegetable like a zucchini. I would happily offer a substitute spice if there was one, but the uniqueness of this dish lies in its really distinctive flavor. You can find amba, also known as mango or amchoor/amchur powder, at most Middle Eastern or Indian supermarkets, or failing that, buy it online. Feel free, however, to use raisins instead of the barberries if you can't find them. This dish goes well with other small plates, such as Caramelized Butternut Squash with Whipped Feta and Zhoug (*see* page 178), Fried Eggplant in Tomato Sauce (*see* page 26), and even Sticky Pomegranate Salmon (*see* page 117).

Amba-spiced Zucchini with Barberries and Labneh

Serves 4

2 tablespoons olive oil

1 white onion, finely diced

2 zucchini, halved lengthwise and sliced

1 teaspoon amba spice (mango or amchoor/amchur powder)

juice of 1 lemon

pinch of salt, if needed

3 heaped tablespoons Labneh (*see* page 47)

3 tablespoons pine nuts, toasted

3 tablespoons dried barberries

Heat the oil in a skillet, add the onion, and gently fry for about 5 minutes until starting to soften. Add the zucchini and the amba spice. Cook for 10 to 15 minutes until the zucchini are cooked through and starting to brown.

Remove the skillet from the heat and season with the lemon juice and the salt if needed.

Spread the labneh onto a serving dish, top with the zucchini, and scatter with the toasted pine nuts and barberries to garnish.

I had to include two stuffed-eggplant recipes in this book because I couldn't decide between this one and the Tomato-stuffed Eggplant with a Sourdough and Walnut Crumb on page 135. While they are both very different, they each celebrate how amazing this vegetable is as a vehicle for some really powerful flavor toppings.

Baba Ganoush-stuffed Eggplant with Tomato and Fennel Confit

Serves 4 as a main or 8 as a side

4 eggplants
½ cup olive oil
16 small cherry tomatoes
2 small fennel bulbs, woody stalks and cores removed and fronds reserved to garnish, very thinly sliced (preferably with a mandoline if you have one)
1 green chile, halved lengthwise
1 tablespoon tahini
juice of ½ lemon
2 garlic cloves, minced
pinch of sea salt
2oz feta cheese
freshly ground black pepper
1 tablespoon mint leaves, finely chopped

Preheat the oven to 350°F.

If you have a gas stove, using a pair of tongs, hold each eggplant one at a time over a high flame to lightly char the skins, turning to ensure that all sides are charred; this will take no more than 5 minutes. Place on a baking pan. If you don't have a gas stove, preheat the broiler to high. Place the eggplants on a baking pan lined with foil and cook for around 10 to 15 minutes, turning halfway through, until the skins have started to blister.

Bake the charred eggplants for 30 minutes until cooked through.

Meanwhile, add the oil to a skillet with the tomatoes, fennel, and green chile, and cook over low heat for about 10 minutes until the tomatoes start to pop their skins and soften.

Remove the eggplants from the oven, and when cool enough to handle, halve them lengthwise and carefully scoop out the flesh, making sure that you leave about a 1/16-inch layer of flesh in the skins. Add the scooped-out flesh to a bowl and mix with the tahini, lemon juice, garlic, and salt.

Return the flesh mixture to the skins, using a slotted spoon to avoid adding excess oil, then spoon the tomato and fennel confit on top.

Crumble the feta cheese on top of the confit, add a grinding of black pepper, and garnish with the chopped mint and reserved fennel fronds. Serve at room temperature.

Schupfnudeln are potato noodles eaten in the same quantity by the Germans as gnocchi are by the Italians. Also known as *fingernudeln* due to their fingerlike shape, the hand-rolled potato dough for these noodles is often made by my kids. They love rolling the dough with their small hands into little worm shapes and making a complete floury mess in the kitchen, but it's the creamy mushroom sauce with the buttery little noodles that they enjoy the most (even though they always claim to hate mushrooms).

Schupfnudeln with Creamy Mushroom Sauce

Serves 4

For the schupfnudeln
2¼lb russet potatoes, scrubbed
1 egg yolk
table salt
½ teaspoon ground white pepper
¼ teaspoon freshly grated nutmeg
2½ cups all-purpose flour, plus extra for dusting
⅓ cup potato flour
1 tablespoon canola oil
2 tablespoons butter, divided

For the creamy mushroom sauce
1 tablespoon canola oil
2 tablespoons butter
2 shallots, finely diced
2 garlic cloves, minced
3½ cups sliced cremino mushrooms
1 tablespoon thyme leaves, very finely chopped, plus 1 teaspoon for garnish
½ cup Madeira wine
1 cup vegetable stock (made using 1 teaspoon bouillon powder)
1¼ cups heavy cream
½ teaspoon sea salt
freshly ground black pepper

Start by making the schupfnudeln. Cook the unpeeled potatoes in a large saucepan of boiling water for 20 to 25 minutes until very tender. Drain and let cool in a colander.

Peel and then mash the potatoes really well so that there are no lumps; a potato ricer would be best for this job.

Add the mashed potatoes to a bowl and mix in the egg yolk, 1 teaspoon of table salt, white pepper, and nutmeg. Then gently work in the flours, being careful not to overmix the ingredients.

Turn the dough out onto a lightly floured work surface and roll into a long sausage shape about ¾ inch thick. Cut into ½-inch thick pieces and then roll each piece into a little pencil-shaped noodle.

Bring a large saucepan of salted water to a boil and add the noodles. As soon as they float to the surface, after approximately a minute, transfer with a slotted spoon to a bowl of iced water.

For the sauce, heat the oil and butter in a large skillet, add the shallots, garlic, and mushrooms and fry over medium heat for around 10 minutes, stirring frequently, until the mushrooms have softened. Add the thyme and cook for a further 2 minutes. Turn the heat up, add the Madeira, and let the mixture bubble away for 5 minutes until the liquid has evaporated and the mushrooms have started to turn golden at the edges. Add the stock and cream and bring to a boil, then continue cooking over medium heat for 8 minutes to reduce and thicken the sauce. Season with the salt and black pepper, cover, and keep warm.

To fry the schupfnudeln, heat the oil in a large skillet and add a small piece of the butter. Fry the noodles, in batches, over medium-high heat for 2 to 3 minutes, shaking them around in the skillet, until they turn golden brown. Remove each fried batch of noodles with a slotted spoon and add a little more butter to the skillet before adding the next batch of noodles.

Divide the noodles among 4 shallow bowls, spoon the mushroom sauce onto each serving, and garnish with the remaining teaspoon of thyme.

Dressings, pickles & sauces

I met a very talented pickle man called Nick Vadasz of Vadasz Deli at my local farmers' market. His Jewish grandmother, who left her native Hungary in the late 1950s, provided the inspiration for his pickling enterprise, and working out of his premises in Hackney, East London, he continues the family tradition by producing an amazing range of pickles, from kimchi to cucumbers. Having tried a few, I asked him very politely for his pickled red cabbage recipe, one of my favorites. To my amazement he kindly agreed, so I am delighted to share it with you. This will make a large quantity, but it keeps for up to 12 weeks in the fridge, and there's no harm in having a regular supply handy.

Pickled Red Cabbage

Makes 4 x 1-quart jars

1 large red cabbage

For the brine
1¼ quarts spirit vinegar
2 cups granulated sugar
½ cup sea salt
2 cups water
3 teaspoons juniper berries, coarsely crushed
2 teaspoons black peppercorns, coarsely crushed
4 teaspoons caraway seeds
4 teaspoons dill seeds

Wash the jars thoroughly and then sterilize by putting them through a cycle in the dishwater or placing them in a large pan of simmering water for about 5 to 10 minutes. Remove with tongs and let drain and dry.

For the brine, put the vinegar, sugar, salt, and measured water into a large stainless steel saucepan and heat gently, stirring occasionally, until the sugar and salt have dissolved. Add all the spices to the hot brine.

Cut the cabbage in half and remove the core, then slice very thinly using a mandoline or food processor, or by hand.

Divide the cabbage between 4 × 1-quart preserving jars, filling each half full. Pour in the hot brine and seal. Let stand at room temperature for 24 hours before transferring to the fridge for 1 to 2 weeks before eating.

Tahini is traditionally regarded as a condiment in the Middle East, much like tomato ketchup in the West, but it can also be used to bring a lovely Middle Eastern flavor to any dish. My fridge is never without a squeezy bottle full of this dressing, ready to drizzle over salads and meats or just to use as a dipping sauce for pretty much anything. The dense sesame paste is lightened here with some yogurt and fresh lemon juice.

Tahini Dressing

Makes 4 servings

⅓ cup tahini
⅓ cup plain yogurt
juice of ½ lemon
½ teaspoon sea salt

Mix the tahini and yogurt together in a bowl, then add the lemon juice and salt and whisk them in.

Thin with water to achieve your desired consistency if using as a salad dressing or dipping sauce.

The dressing will keep in the fridge for up to 5 days, sealed in an airtight container.

Chrain holds a very poignant memory for me. One Seder night, the ritual feast that marks the start of Passover, my older sister and some very close family friends decided to play a trick on me. They told me (sorry, dared me) to take a large spoon of chrain and eat it on its own. Never one to pass up a dare, I did it, and when my face went as many shades of deep red as the chrain, they rolled around laughing, with the parents joining in, too. I have still to this day never lived it down. Some 30 years later when I find myself making this very hot and tear-jerking condiment, I can't help but smile. This fiery red horseradish and beet combo is a particularly good accompaniment to Fried Fish Balls (*see* page 59) or cold meats.

Chrain

Serves 8

2oz piece fresh horseradish root, peeled and chopped into chunks

1 red beet, around ¼lb, peeled and chopped into large pieces

2 teaspoons white wine vinegar

1 tablespoon fresh lemon juice

1 tablespoon superfine sugar

1 teaspoon sea salt

freshly ground black pepper

Add the horseradish to a power blender and blend on the highest speed until it is almost like a paste.

Add the beet and blend again on high speed until completely chopped.

Add the remaining ingredients and give the mixture a final blitz, then taste (with a lot of caution!) to check for seasoning.

Transfer to a sterilized jar (*see* page 144) or airtight container, seal, and store in the fridge until ready to serve. The chrain will keep for up to 4 weeks.

One of my greatest food experiences was traveling to Stockholm to cook in two of the country's most dynamic and cutting-edge restaurants. Sweden's cuisine sings to my heart with its pickles, curing, smoking, marinating—all the culinary techniques I love and want to learn more about. Given the very short summer season in Sweden, pickling is essential as a way of preserving the vegetables that have limited time to grow. The first thing I learned was how to make a classic pickling liquid and I've now adopted this recipe for all manner of vegetables, including fennel, radish, and red onions. Attika vinegar is available through specialist online suppliers, but you could use a different spirit vinegar (not malt vinegar) as a substitute.

Sweet Pickled Beets

Makes 3 x 9-ounce jars

2¼lb beets
¾ cup Attika vinegar or spirit vinegar
1½ cups superfine sugar
2¾ cups water

Wash and sterilize the jars (*see* page 144).

Remove the stalks from the beets and scrub well. Add to a saucepan and cover with cold water. Bring to a boil, then reduce the heat and let simmer gently for around 25 minutes or until the point of a sharp knife goes in easily, depending on the size of the beet.

Drain and let cool, then carefully remove the skins with the back of a table knife. Chop into small cubes.

Put the vinegar, sugar, and measured water into a large stainless steel saucepan and heat gently, stirring occasionally, until the sugar has dissolved. Let cool completely.

Divide the beet cubes between 3 × 9-ounce preserving jars, add the pickling liquid, and seal. The beets are ready to eat right away, or can be kept for up to 3 months in the fridge.

When I was growing up, our fridge was always full of pickles, as they were part of our everyday condiments on the table for lunch and dinner. They were always Mrs. Elswood ready-made pickles from the kosher section; my mom never thought about making her own. Given the vast quantity of cucumbers that my own family consumes, sheer economics led me on a quest to devise my own quick-and-easy concoction. The small Lebanese or Turkish cucumbers work so much better than English cucumbers because they are less watery and hold their crunch better. They can be found in any ethnic supermarket.

Dill Pickles

Makes 2 x 1-quart jars

¾ cup distilled white vinegar

3 tablespoons sea salt

3 tablespoons superfine sugar

1¼ cups cold water

8 small Lebanese or Turkish cucumbers, halved lengthwise

4 large garlic cloves, peeled and halved

1½ tablespoons coriander seeds

1½ teaspoons mustard seeds

10 sprigs of dill

Wash and sterilize the jars (see page 144).

Put the vinegar, salt, and sugar in a medium stainless steel saucepan and gently heat, stirring, until the sugar and salt have dissolved. Transfer the liquid to a bowl and whisk in the measured cold water. Let the brine cool, then refrigerate until needed.

Divide the cucumbers between 2 × 1-quart preserving jars, tall enough to hold the cucumber spears vertically, and then add the garlic, coriander and mustard seeds, and the dill sprigs. Pour the brine equally over the cucumbers, topping off with cold water if necessary to cover the cucumbers.

Seal the jars and let stand in the fridge for 24 hours before eating. They will keep for up to a month.

Sides & salads

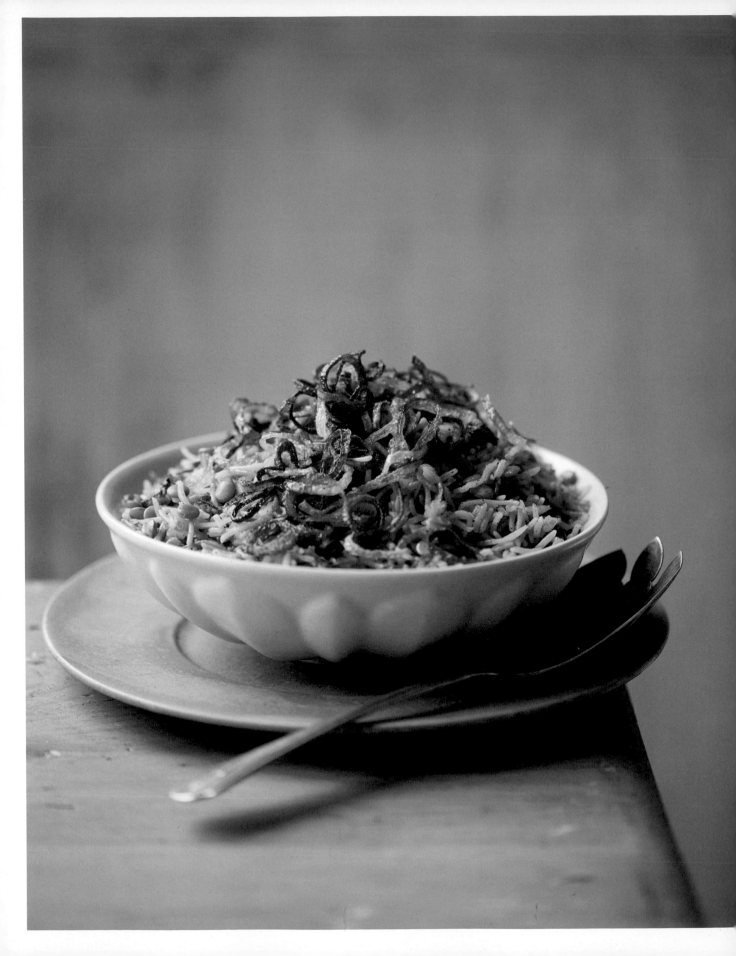

This is the dish that I get asked to make all the time, so it seemed only fitting that I included this in my first ever signature offering on *MasterChef*. Thankfully, it was a triumph. Better known as an Egyptian peasant dish, the warm, comforting notes of the Lebanese spices and the hearty nature of the lentils make a little of this stretch a long way. It will stand as a meal in its own right accompanied by a simple cumin-spiced yogurt and a bowl of Israeli "Chik Chak" Salad (*see* page 172), or for a special occasion I normally serve it with Lamb Ghormeh Sabzi (*see* page 92) and Tzimmes (*see* page 177). The caramelized onions are the highlight of this dish and I use flour to turn them a bit crispy, but feel free to omit it if you have a wheat intolerance; they will still be just as tasty.

Sephardi Rice with Vermicelli and Lentils

Serves 6 to 8

1 cup dried green lentils

2 tablespoons all-purpose flour (optional)

sea salt

3 large onions, sliced into thin half-moons

¼ cup olive oil

½ stick unsalted butter

⅔ cup dried short vermicelli egg noodles

1½ cups basmati rice

2 teaspoons Lebanese 7-spice Mix (*see* page 14)

2½ cups hot chicken or vegetable stock

vegetable oil, for deep-frying

2 shallots, sliced into thin rings, to garnish

freshly ground black pepper

Rinse the lentils really well, then place in a saucepan, cover with plenty of cold water, and bring to a boil. Cover with a lid, reduce the heat, and let simmer for 20 to 25 minutes, checking after 15 minutes; the lentils should be cooked but not mushy. Drain and refresh under cold running water to stop any further cooking, then set aside.

Meanwhile, if using the flour, season with 1 teaspoon salt and spread out on a plate, then toss the onion slices in the seasoned flour to coat. Heat the olive oil in a large skillet and gently fry the onions, in batches, for about 25 minutes until a rich dark brown color. Remove with a slotted spoon and transfer to a plate lined with paper towels to drain.

Heat the butter in a large, heavy saucepan with a lid, and when it is sizzling, add the vermicelli, stirring constantly until it is just starting to brown. Add the rice and Lebanese 7-spice mix and stir everything together until the rice is nicely coated in the butter, then add the hot stock and bring to a boil. Cover and let cook on the lowest heat possible for exactly 12 minutes. Turn the heat off, remove the lid, and cover the pan with a clean dish cloth. Replace the lid and let the covered pan sit for 10 minutes, to help fluff up the grains.

For the garnish, pour the vegetable oil into a small, deep saucepan and add the shallots while the pan is still cold. Heat the oil; once it reaches a temperature of around 340°F, the shallots will crisp quite quickly, so stay near the pan. When they are golden brown, remove with a slotted spoon and transfer to a plate lined with paper towels to drain.

Add the lentils to the rice, then the caramelized onions and stir through with 2 forks to stop the rice from clumping together. Season with extra salt, if needed, and some black pepper. Tip the rice mixture into a large bowl and garnish with the crispy shallots.

My mother-in-law is one of nine siblings: seven brothers and two sisters. While two of her brothers came to live in the UK, the remaining three brothers and her sister stayed in Israel, and it's those siblings and their children who we make a concerted effort to go and see every other year with the kids. The thing I look forward to the most is the food. Whether it's a giant barbecue, a traditional High Holiday feast, or just a Friday night dinner, the discussions around what we are going to eat, followed by who is going to make it and where we are eating, take a considerable amount of time and effort. The results are always sensational, and a few loosened belt notches later, I will inevitably be found following the chief cook around with my pen and paper, making note of the recipes. This was one of those that I scribbled down. First made for me by Aunty Rochele at my engagement party, this dish has been the talking point at just about every barbecue or buffet spread I've offered it up at ever since. It's very easy to make with just a few simple ingredients, and goes really well with the Tomato-stuffed Eggplant with a Sourdough and Walnut Crumb (*see* page 135) or the Chicken and Pistachio Meatballs with Cilantro Tahini (*see* page 85).

Wild Rice Salad

Serves 6 as a main or 8 to 10 as a side

1½ cups wild rice

1¼ cups long-grain rice

1 tablespoon sunflower oil, divided

20 ripe cherry tomatoes, halved

⅔ cup raw cashews

1 cup sun-dried tomatoes in oil, chopped into bite-sized pieces, plus some of the oil

½ cup halved pitted green olives

2 large handfuls of basil leaves, finely chopped

sea salt and freshly ground black pepper

Rinse the wild rice and add to a large saucepan with about 4 cups of salted boiling water. Boil for around 40 to 45 minutes, checking to ensure that the grains have popped but still retain some bite.

While the wild rice is cooking, rinse the long-grain rice and add to a separate large saucepan with about 1¼ quarts boiling water and a pinch of salt. Cover the pan and cook over low heat for around 12 to 15 minutes or until cooked but still slightly al dente. Drain the rice and let cool.

Heat 1 teaspoon of the oil in a skillet, add the cherry tomatoes, and cook over high heat for a couple of minutes or until they just start to break down at the edges. Remove from the pan and set aside. Add the cashews to the pan and fry until they just start to color slightly, then set aside.

To assemble the salad, mix the cooked wild and long-grain rice together in a large bowl, then add the sun-dried tomatoes and olives, using a few drops of the oil from the tomatoes to coat the salad slightly. Add the chopped basil and season to taste with sea salt and black pepper. Serve at room temperature.

A lovely and very talented friend of mine, Nikita Gulhane, runs the Spice Monkey Indian cookery school in North London and once offered this rice dish as part of an incredible lunch spread. I had just had my first baby and we were gathering for our prenatal-class moms' (and sometimes dads') weekly get-together. I hadn't cooked for a while and was desperate to find tasty and easy meals I could prepare while juggling the demands of a small and needy child. This spicy mushroom rice was the most adventurous dish I could muster while caring for my newborn baby. Nikita told me what ingredients he used and I then went away and constructed a recipe from it. Minimal fuss; maximum taste. This is great served with the Turmeric-battered Cauliflower with Chile and Saffron Yogurt (*see* page 168).

Spicy Mushroom and Cashew Rice

Serves 4

1 tablespoon vegetable oil
1½ teaspoons cumin seeds
½ teaspoon ground turmeric
½ teaspoon dried red chile flakes
thumb-sized piece of fresh ginger root, peeled and finely chopped
1 small white onion, minced
1 fat garlic clove, minced
2 cups sliced cremino mushrooms
⅓ cup raw cashews, halved
1 cup basmati rice
1¾ cups boiling water
1 teaspoon sea salt
freshly ground black pepper

Heat the oil in a saucepan over medium heat, add the cumin seeds, turmeric, chile flakes, and ginger and cook, stirring, for a couple of minutes. Then add the onion and cook with the spices until it is softened. Add the garlic, mushrooms, and cashews and cook for a few more minutes, then tip in the rice and stir, making sure that the grains are nicely coated in the oil and spices.

Pour in the measured boiling water and season with the salt and a few grindings of black pepper. Bring to a boil, cover with the lid, reduce the heat to its lowest setting, and let cook for 10 minutes.

Turn the heat off and let the rice stand, with the lid on, to steam for a further 10 minutes before serving.

These are definitely what you would call special occasion potatoes. The recipe is a Lebanese take on my father-in-law's little crispy fried potatoes, and works really well as an accompaniment to a robust meat such as lamb or beef.

Potatoes Fried with Chile and Cilantro

Serves 6

6 large white russet potatoes, peeled and cut into small cubes

½ cup vegetable or sunflower oil

1 red onion, finely diced

2 garlic cloves, minced

1 red chile, seeded and finely chopped (leave the seeds in if you want more heat)

1 teaspoon ground coriander

½ teaspoon ground cumin

2 large handfuls of fresh cilantro, finely chopped

sea salt and freshly ground black pepper

Blanch the potatoes in a large saucepan of salted boiling water for 5 minutes. Drain and let dry.

If your skillet isn't large enough to hold the potatoes in a single layer, do this next step in batches; just divide up the oil. Heat the oil over medium-high heat, and when it has almost reached smoking point, carefully add the potatoes (wear an apron and stand well back) and fry for around 10 minutes, turning every so often, so that they color evenly.

Add the onion, garlic, chile, and spices, season with sea salt and black pepper, and fry for a further 5 minutes until the potatoes are nicely crisp and golden and cooked through. Finish by adding the fresh cilantro (reserving a little for garnish) and stir through. Serve the potatoes hot, garnished with the reserved cilantro.

Tip

If I'm cooking for spice-averse kids as well, I divide the amount of potatoes I've blanched in half and roast their half in sunflower oil in a roasting pan in an oven preheated to 400°F for around 30 minutes, turning frequently.

I used to enjoy latkes every Hanukkah, when they are traditionally served to symbolize the miracle of oil (yes, oily foods are the done thing during this festival), along with cheese blintzes and doughnuts. The key to achieving the perfect latke is to make sure the oil is not so hot that the potato burns before it is properly cooked, but hot enough that it crisps up nicely. The topping choices are vast and include Salt Beef (*see* page 106) and pickles or Lox (*see* page 39) and sour cream. Alternatively, simply enjoy them on their own, snatched quickly out of the pan and eaten between pieces of paper towels the way I did.

Fennel and Potato Latkes with Lemon and Chive Aïoli

Makes 20 latkes

1 fennel bulb
4 white potatoes, about 2¼lb in total
1 onion
2 teaspoons fennel seeds, crushed with a mortar and pestle
3 large eggs, beaten
⅔ cup all-purpose flour or medium matzo meal
2 teaspoons sea salt
freshly ground black pepper
½ cup sunflower oil, for frying, divided

For the lemon and chive aïoli
⅓ cup mayonnaise
juice of ½ lemon
1 garlic clove, crushed
1 tablespoon finely snipped chives

Preheat the oven to 225°F.

Cut the woody stalk off the fennel bulb, then cut the bulb in half lengthwise. Remove the core and slice very thinly, preferably with a mandoline if you have one. Add the fennel slices to a bowl of cold water and let soften for 10 minutes.

Peel the potatoes and grate coarsely or, even better, use the grating attachment on your food processor if you have one. Peel and grate the onion, then add with the potato to a clean dish cloth and squeeze as much of the liquid out as possible.

Add the potato and onion to a large bowl. Drain the fennel and add to the bowl with the crushed fennel seeds, eggs, flour or matzo meal, salt, and some black pepper. Mix really well with your hands.

Heat ⅓ cup of the oil in a large skillet over medium heat. When the oil is hot but not smoking, add about 3 tablespoonfuls of the mixture per latke to the pan and flatten with a spatula. Fry the latkes, turning them over once, for around 4 to 5 minutes on each side until a deep golden brown. Remove with a slotted spoon to a baking pan lined with paper towels and keep warm in the oven while you fry the rest. Repeat with the remaining latke mixture, adding a bit more of the remaining oil each time.

Meanwhile, mix all the ingredients for the aïoli together well in a bowl.

Serve the latkes warm on a large plate with a bowl of the aïoli on the side.

Tip
You can store any leftover latkes in a single layer on a baking pan in the fridge and then reheat in an oven preheated to 400°F for 20 to 30 minutes.

This is a lovely twist on a classic potato salad and it's my barbecue or picnic table staple. The crunch and sharpness from the spicy cucumber pairs really nicely with the soft creamy potatoes and egg. You will find the Beit Hashita Cucumbers in most major supermarkets in the kosher section or at Middle Eastern grocery stores, but if you can't get these, any type of pickled cucumber or cornichon would work well.

New Potato and Egg Salad with Spicy Cucumbers

Serves 8

2¼lb baby new potatoes, scrubbed
4 hard-boiled eggs
6 Beit Hashita Cucumbers in Brine or other pickled cucumbers (or use 12 cornichons)
1 teaspoon sea salt
freshly ground black pepper
6 scallions, thinly sliced
¼ to ⅓ cup good-quality mayonnaise

Cook the potatoes in a large saucepan of boiling water for approximately 12 to 15 minutes until cooked through. Drain and let cool, then scrape off the skins. Halve any larger potatoes so that you end up with them all about the same size.

Shell and coarsely chop the eggs and cucumbers into dice, then add to a large bowl with the salt and some black pepper, the scallions (reserving a few slices for garnish), and mayonnaise. Add the potatoes and mix well.

Serve the salad garnished with the reserved scallions and a couple of extra grindings of black pepper.

Tips

* I prefer to buy small new potatoes and cook them in their skins for extra flavor, then scrape off the skins once cooled, but you can of course leave the skins on to reduce the work involved a little; the result is equally tasty.

* For an extra flavor punch, add a crushed large garlic clove to the mayo.

Cauliflower is having what you would call "a moment," with many menus now offering it as a dish in its own right, elevating it from humble side vegetable to queen of the plate. Its versatility makes it a great vegetable to experiment with, and that's exactly what I was doing when this recipe came about. Fried, roasted, baked, mashed, or blitzed into couscous, it's like a flavor sponge, gracefully accepting whatever dressing you throw on it. As a cook, I often think of flavor first, texture second, and visual impact third. This dish is the perfect result of the three: the tenderness of the cauliflower with the earthy and slightly tangy flavor of the za'atar and barberries, against the soft couscous and crunchy almonds. Enjoy this as a hearty lunch or supper. If you struggle to find barberries, you can replace them with dried cranberries, raisins, or dried sour cherries.

Pan-fried Cauliflower with Caramelized Red Onions, Toasted Israeli Couscous, and Almonds

Serves 6

⅓ cup olive oil, divided

1 large red onion, thinly sliced into half-moons

2 tablespoons soft dark brown sugar

2 tablespoons balsamic vinegar

1 large or 2 small cauliflowers, cut into large florets, any small leaves retained

1 cup toasted Israeli couscous (or substitute fregola if you can't find it)

2 cups hot chicken or vegetable stock

3 tablespoons butter, cut into pieces

2 to 3 tablespoons Za'atar (see page 15)

1 tablespoon Lebanese 7-spice Mix (see page 14)

1 cup raw unblanched almonds

⅓ cup pine nuts, lightly toasted

2 large handfuls of dried barberries

sea salt and freshly ground black pepper

To garnish
generous sprinkling of pomegranate seeds

a few oregano leaves

Heat 2 tablespoons of the oil in a skillet, add the onion, and gently fry for 10 to 15 minutes with a pinch of salt until caramelized, stirring occasionally. Add the sugar and vinegar and cook for 5 to 10 minutes more until slightly sticky.

Meanwhile, blanch the cauliflower and its leaves in a large saucepan of salted boiling water for 3 to 4 minutes. Drain and let steam-dry in a colander.

Heat a tablespoon of the remaining oil in a saucepan over medium heat, add the couscous, and stir to coat. Fry for around 2 to 3 minutes, then cover with the hot stock and add a pinch of salt. Bring to a boil, then cover and simmer for around 8 to 10 minutes. Drain off any liquid and set aside.

Heat the remaining oil in a skillet over medium heat, add the cauliflower and fry, turning occasionally, for 10 minutes or until golden and cooked through. Drain any oil out of the pan and set the cauliflower aside.

Place the pan back on the heat and add the butter, za'atar, and Lebanese spice mix. Stir until the butter has melted, then return the cauliflower to the pan and baste until well coated. Add the almonds, pine nuts, and barberries and stir everything in the pan until it has all heated through.

Transfer the cauliflower mixture to a large bowl and mix through the couscous and the cooked red onion. Season with some sea salt and black pepper, and garnish with the pomegranate seeds and oregano leaves. The dish can be served hot or at room temperature.

Tip

The couscous and onion can be made up to 24 hours ahead and the cauliflower blanched in advance, so don't worry about having to tackle all the elements at the same time.

Crispy and lightly spiced, this dish makes a lovely sharing plate for an appetizer, or a pre-dinner nibble. You want the cauliflower florets to be bite-sized, but not so small that they can't take on the batter.

Turmeric-battered Cauliflower with Chile and Saffron Yogurt

Serves 4

1 cauliflower, cut into florets
vegetable or canola oil, for deep-frying

For the yogurt
small pinch of saffron threads
3 tablespoons hot water
1 cup Greek yogurt
juice of ½ lemon
¼ teaspoon Aleppo pepper
1 garlic clove, crushed
pinch of sea salt

For the batter
1 tablespoon nigella seeds
1 tablespoon ground turmeric
1⅓ cups all-purpose flour sifted with 1 teaspoon baking powder
1 cup chilled sparkling water
1 teaspoon table salt

For the garnish
handful of picked cilantro leaves, coarsely chopped
1 tablespoon pomegranate molasses

Blanch the cauliflower in a large saucepan of salted boiling water for 2 minutes, then drain in a colander and refresh under cold running water to stop any further cooking.

For the yogurt, infuse the saffron in the measured hot water for 20 minutes, then strain out the saffron and discard. Mix the saffron water into the yogurt and add the remaining yogurt ingredients. Cover and refrigerate until ready to serve.

Heat the oil for deep-frying in a deep-fat fryer or medium saucepan (ensure that the oil is a minimum of 2 inches deep, but don't fill the pan more than halfway) and place over medium heat to heat up to about 340°F.

Meanwhile, beat all the ingredients for the batter together in a bowl until you have a thick consistency.

Test the temperature of the oil by dropping in a little of the batter—if it sizzles, the oil is ready. Dip the cauliflower florets in the batter to coat, shaking off the excess, and fry, in small batches, for 4 minutes. Remove with a slotted spoon and transfer to a plate lined with paper towels.

Transfer to a serving plate and garnish with the cilantro and pomegranate molasses, with the yogurt on the side for dipping.

The season for these delicious little morsels is annoyingly short, so I make the most of them during their brief winter appearance. This recipe was born out of one of many experimental sessions trying to find a suitable partner for them. In this case, crisp green beans and some gently cooked red onions did the job really well; add to that the creamy tarragon dressing and it's mouth-wateringly good. I've served this as an appetizer for my supper clubs to high acclaim, and it's sure to convert anyone repelled by Jerusalem artichokes' rather intimidating appearance into cooking with them.

Roasted Jerusalem Artichokes and Green Bean Salad

Serves 6

1lb 2oz Jerusalem artichokes
⅓ cup olive oil, divided
2 tablespoons lemon thyme leaves (or 2 teaspoons dried thyme if you can't get hold of it)
1 large red onion, thinly sliced into half-moons
7oz green beans
5½oz pea shoots or watercress
sea salt

For the dressing
3 black garlic cloves, peeled
⅓ cup heavy cream
2 tablespoons fresh lemon juice
2 tablespoons finely chopped tarragon
freshly ground black pepper

Preheat the oven to 350°F.

Scrub the artichokes really well and remove any knobbly parts. Cut into wedges and place on a baking pan with 3 tablespoons of the olive oil, the thyme, and a teaspoon of salt, tossing everything together really well to ensure that everything is coated in the oil. Roast for 25 to 30 minutes, then increase the heat to 400°F and roast for a further 10 minutes until cooked through and golden, turning them over 2 or 3 times during the process. Remove from the oven and let cool slightly.

Warm the remaining 3 tablespoons of olive oil in a skillet, add the onion with a pinch of salt, and cook over really low heat for about 10 minutes until soft and translucent. Set aside.

Cook the green beans in a saucepan of salted boiling water for around 3 minutes until just al dente, then drain and refresh under cold running water to stop any further cooking.

To make the dressing, pound the black garlic into a paste using a mortar and pestle or with the back of a spoon. Mix the garlic into the cream and whisk with the remaining dressing ingredients, reserving a little of the tarragon for garnish, then season with a few good grindings of black pepper and set aside.

To assemble the salad, place the pea shoots or watercress on a plate, arrange the artichokes, onion, and green beans nicely on to, and drizzle generously with the dressing. Garnish with the reserved tarragon and serve.

Tip

This salad is best served at room temperature, so make everything ahead but don't dress it until just before you are ready to serve. If you can't find black garlic, the dressing will taste almost as good without it.

This salad is served for breakfast, lunch, and dinner in Israel, in every home, restaurant, market, and café. I first learned the art of chopping (yes, that's the only skill required here) this salad while working on a kibbutz aged 19 in the far north of Israel. Working in the kitchen was a job reserved for the residents (kibbutzniks) only, not the working guests, but I pretty much begged to help out one day and this was the task I was given—chopping enough vegetables for a salad to feed 200 people. I loved every minute, setting myself the challenge of chopping each vegetable as uniformly and precisely as possible. That is the art here, making sure all the vegetables are the same size and nice and small. See this as a therapeutic job and not a chore, and you will enjoy it so much more.

Israeli "Chik Chak" Salad

Serves 4 as a side

1 whole cucumber

6 ripe plum tomatoes or ½lb baby plum tomatoes

¼lb radishes

½ yellow bell pepper

⅔ cup green olives stuffed with jalapeño (I like Fragata) or pimento

½ red onion

For the dressing

juice of 1 lemon (squeeze over half to begin with, then add the remainder if needed)

3 tablespoons good-quality extra virgin olive oil, plus extra if needed

½ teaspoon sea salt

freshly ground black pepper (be generous)

1 teaspoon ground sumac

Split the cucumber in half lengthwise and remove the seeds. Cut the tomatoes in half and scoop out the seeds (if you are using baby plum tomatoes, you don't need to remove the seeds). Trim the radishes and core and seed the bell pepper.

Dice all the vegetables the same size and as small as you possibly can.

Add to a bowl with all the dressing ingredients, then add more oil and lemon juice if needed; you want it to be nice and sharp.

Serve with just about anything.

Halloumi is one of my favorite cheeses and za'atar is one of my favorite spices, so it felt only right to put the two together. I always dust the halloumi slices with cornstarch so that they immediately form a crust when they hit the hot skillet. This is a simple yet really delicious salad that makes an impressive vegetarian appetizer, or a lovely addition to a buffet spread.

Za'atar-crusted Halloumi Salad with a Lime and Mint Dressing

Serves 4

1 large fennel bulb, woody stalk removed, and very thinly sliced (preferably with a mandoline if you have one)
1 heaped tablespoon cornstarch
2 tablespoons Za'atar (*see* page 15)
10½oz halloumi cheese
I tablespoon olive oil
seeds from ½ pomegranate, to garnish

For the dressing
⅓ cup olive oil
1 teaspoon white balsamic vinegar
juice of 1 lime
10 mint leaves, finely chopped
2 teaspoons Za'atar (*see* page 15)
pinch of sea salt
freshly ground black pepper

Place the sliced fennel in a bowl, cover with cold water, and let soften for 10 minutes, then drain.

Mix the cornstarch and za'atar together on a plate, then spread out. Slice the halloumi and roll in the seasoned flour to coat.

Heat the olive oil in a skillet over high heat, and when it is really hot, add the halloumi and fry, undisturbed, for 1 to 2 minutes. Then turn the cheese over and cook on the other side for a further minute. Transfer to a plate.

Add all the ingredients for the dressing, reserving some of the mint for garnish, to a bowl or, even better, a jar with screw-top lid and give them a good whisk or securely screw the lid on and shake to combine.

Add the fennel slices to a shallow bowl, set the halloumi on top, and drizzle with the dressing. Garnish with the reserved mint and the pomegranate seeds and serve immediately.

Tzimmes is a classic High Holiday dish, most traditionally eaten on Passover and Rosh Hashanah, and there are dozens of variations above and beyond the carrot and cinnamon version that I've given here. My mom used to make this dish in an attempt to get my sisters and me to eat carrots. Dressing them up in lots of butter and cinnamon certainly helps, but throw in some raisins and then you're talking. For this recipe, I felt it was sweet enough without the addition of any dried fruit, but feel free to add them if you're trying to lure in fussy kids. This is great served with Friday Night Chicken with Onions and Roast Potatoes (*see* page 79).

Tzimmes

Serves 4

2 tablespoons canola oil

1 white onion, thinly sliced

1 teaspoon freshly grated nutmeg

1 teaspoon ground cinnamon

1 teaspoon fennel seeds

½ teaspoon sea salt

4 large carrots, peeled and cut lengthwise, then chopped into half disks about ½ inch thick

2 tablespoons butter

1¼ cups water

grated zest and juice of 1 orange

2 tablespoons date syrup

1 red chile, seeded and finely chopped

1 tablespoon finely chopped flat-leaf parsley

juice of ½ lemon

Heat the oil in a wide, heavy saucepan, add the onion, nutmeg, cinnamon, fennel seeds, and salt and sauté over medium heat for about 10 minutes until the onion is soft and translucent. Stir in the carrots and butter and cook for 2 minutes.

Add the measured water, orange zest and juice, and date syrup, cover with a lid, and cook for 30 minutes or until the carrots are soft.

Take the lid off and cook for a further 5 minutes to reduce the liquid into a syrupy mass.

Add the chile, parsley, and lemon juice to finish before serving.

Sweet, salty, and spicy all on one plate; this dish is a great hit of powerful flavors that all mesh really well together. *Zhoug* is a fiery Middle Eastern relish that works as a condiment for all manner of dishes, so store any leftover sauce in an airtight container in the fridge for up to two weeks.

Caramelized Butternut Squash with Whipped Feta and Zhoug

Serves 4

1 large butternut squash, peeled, seeded, and cut into ¾-inch chunks

2 tablespoons butter, melted

1 tablespoon soft dark brown sugar

1 teaspoon ground cinnamon

½ teaspoon sea salt

¼ cup unsalted pistachio nuts

½ cup Whipped Feta (*see* page 46)

For the zhoug

1 bunch of cilantro, including stalks

½ bunch of flat-leaf parsley, stalks removed

1 green chile

1 tablespoon dried red chile flakes

½ teaspoon ground cumin

½ teaspoon ground coriander

½ teaspoon sea salt

½ cup canola oil

juice of ½ lemon

Preheat the oven to 400°F.

Place the butternut squash in a bowl and toss with the melted butter, sugar, cinnamon, and salt. Spread out the coated squash pieces on a baking pan and roast for 30 minutes, or until cooked through and the sugar is starting to caramelize.

While the squash is roasting, spread out the pistachios on a separate baking pan and roast for 8 minutes or until they begin to brown and smell nutty. Remove from the oven and let cool, then chop coarsely with a knife.

For the zhoug, place all the ingredients except the lemon juice in a food processor and pulse until it forms a loose green sauce. Stir in the lemon juice.

Once cooked, transfer the butternut squash to a serving dish and dot it with tablespoonfuls of the whipped feta before drizzling with the spicy zhoug and scattering with the chopped nuts.

This is a very quick and easy salad to prepare and is a perfect accompaniment to cold meats, salmon, or as part of a meze platter. Although this salad can be served immediately, it's much better left in the fridge for a few hours to allow the onion to soften a little and for the flavors to develop. It goes perfectly with Lox (*see* page 39), or serve as part of a spread with Chopped Liver (*see* page 63), or Egg and Onion (*see* page 62).

Hungarian Cucumber Salad

Serves 4

2 large green cucumbers
1 large white onion, very thinly sliced
1 teaspoon table salt
3 tablespoons superfine sugar
⅓ cup white wine or apple cider vinegar
3 tablespoons water
large handful of dill, finely chopped

Trim and thinly slice the cucumbers, then add to a large bowl along with the onion and salt. Toss together and let sit for 10 minutes.

Add the sugar, vinegar, measured water, and dill to the bowl, then mix all the ingredients together, ensuring that everything is well combined.

Cover and chill in the fridge for a few hours or longer (it only gets better) until you are ready to serve.

I would love to think of a way to make this sound more appetizing than "cabbage salad"—it doesn't exactly jump off the page and scream, "Make me!" But it really is one of the tastiest cabbage salads you will ever eat. With no more than five ingredients, I guarantee you will have your guests clamoring for the recipe. I've kept this guarded for 14 years, ever since I pried the recipe out of my husband's Israeli aunt after she made the dish for our engagement party. I now feel the need to share; some things are too good to keep to yourself.

Aunty Rochele's Cabbage Salad

Serves 8 as part of a meze spread

1 large white cabbage
¼ cup balsamic vinegar
¼ cup soft dark brown sugar
¼ cup soy sauce
¼ cup sunflower oil
3 tablespoons sesame seeds
½ cup pine nuts

Shred the cabbage finely—the grating attachment on your food processor will do the job nicely if you have one. Rinse and set aside to drain; you want it dry before you add the dressing.

Heat the vinegar, sugar, and soy sauce slowly in a saucepan until the sugar has dissolved, then let cool before adding the sunflower oil.

Transfer the cabbage to a large bowl, add the dressing, and give it a good stir—this can sit for a while to allow the flavors to meld before you serve.

Heat a dry skillet, add the sesame seeds and pine nuts, and toast over medium heat until lightly golden and fragrant, shaking the pan constantly. Set aside and add to the salad just before serving.

This is a simple, tasty, and great-looking colorful dish to adorn any buffet table. The earthiness of the beets stands up really well against the cabbage, and paired with the mustardy tang of the dressing, it's a lovely accompaniment to Salt Beef (*see* page 106) and Fennel and Potato Latkes (*see* page 162). In fact, I served this exact combo for one of my supper clubs and it was a real winner among the guests.

Red Cabbage, Black Olive, and Beet Coleslaw

Serves 8

1 red cabbage
2 red beets, peeled
1 cup sliced pitted black olives

For the dressing
1 cup crème fraîche or sour cream
1 tablespoon Dijon mustard
1 small red onion, minced
2 tablespoons balsamic vinegar
1 tablespoon date syrup
½ teaspoon sea salt
freshly ground black pepper

Cut the cabbage in half and remove the core, then shred finely—use the grating attachment on your food processor if you have one. Grate the beets on the large holes of a box grater and combine with the cabbage in a large bowl. Add the sliced olives and set aside.

Beat all the ingredients for the dressing together in a bowl, cover, and let stand in the fridge for around 20 minutes to allow the flavors to mesh.

Add the dressing to the slaw just before serving and toss through.

This dish is inspired by a lovely Mediterranean restaurant close to where I live where they offer something very similar on the menu. Although the tapenade is a combination of bold flavors, it nevertheless allows this wonderful green vegetable to be the star of the plate. You can serve this side dish hot or cold, so it's an ideal prepare-ahead option.

Broccolini with Black Olive Tapenade

Serves 4

½lb broccolini

2 small garlic cloves, peeled

1 cup pitted black olives

2 tablespoons capers

juice of ½ lemon, or to taste

small handful of flat-leaf parsley, finely chopped

freshly ground black pepper

3 tablespoons good-quality extra virgin olive oil, divided, plus extra for drizzling

Blanch the broccolini in a saucepan of boiling water for 90 seconds, then drain and set aside.

Finely chop the garlic, olives, and capers together (a mezzaluna is a really great tool to use here if you have one). Add to a bowl with the lemon juice, parsley, a few grindings of black pepper, and 2 tablespoons of the olive oil. Taste and adjust the seasoning, and if necessary add more lemon juice.

Heat a skillet over medium-high heat, add the remaining tablespoon of oil, and quickly flash-fry the broccolini until it is heated through; you want to ensure that it still retains a bite, so don't overcook it.

Place the broccolini on a plate, top with the tapenade, and drizzle generously with the extra virgin olive oil.

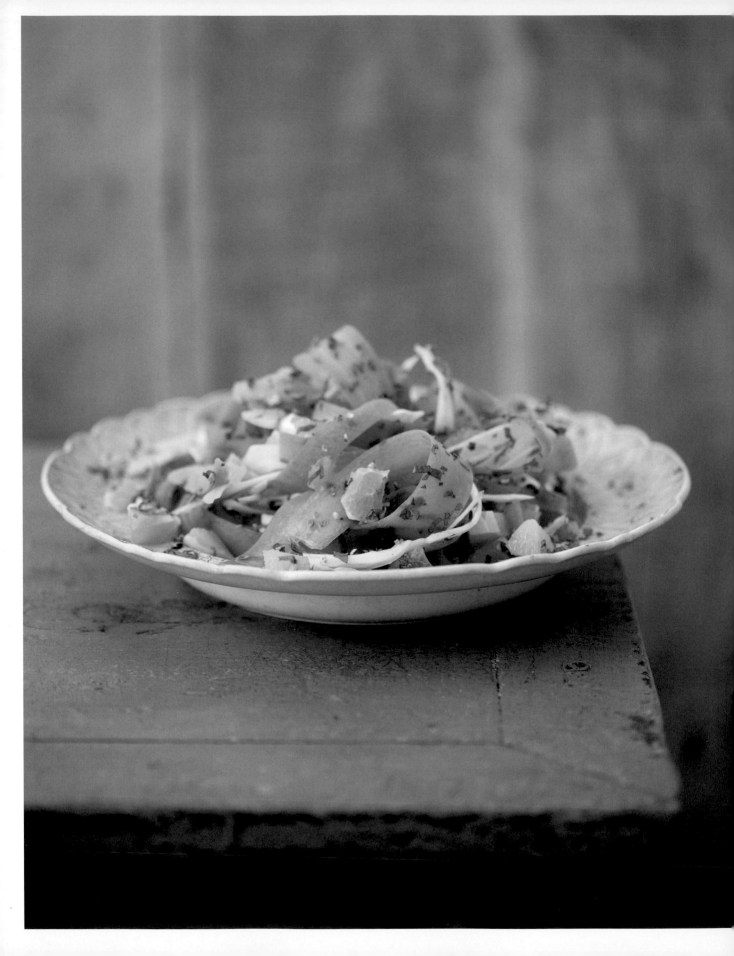

My husband and I united over our love of food, although it was actually our mutual dislike of certain combinations that made us realize how much we had in common. Fruit with savory was the biggest offender, yet here I am promoting the one salad that made me reconsider my food demons. It's lovely and light, making a fantastic accompaniment to my Salmon and Sweet Potato Fishcakes (*see* page 119) and Spiced Cod Falafel (*see* page 43).

Fennel, Orange, and Carrot Salad

Serves 4

1 fennel bulb, cut in half lengthwise and very thinly sliced (preferably with a mandoline if you have one)

1 teaspoon coriander seeds

2 carrots, peeled and shaved into strips with a vegetable peeler

1 orange, peeled, segmented, and cut into small chunks

handful of mint leaves, finely chopped

1 tablespoon extra virgin olive oil

juice of ½ lime

sea salt and freshly ground black pepper

Place the sliced fennel in a bowl, cover with cold water, and let soften for 10 minutes, then drain.

Place a dry pan over medium heat, add the coriander seeds, and toast until they start to smell fragrant, shaking the pan constantly. Grind to a coarse powder with a mortar and pestle.

Transfer the drained fennel to a large bowl, add the carrots, orange, mint leaves, and coriander seeds and toss together. Dress the salad with the oil, lime juice, and salt and black pepper to taste before serving.

Inspiration for this salad came from a very traditional Jewish dish called *kasha varnishkes*. Otherwise known as buckwheat, kasha is a gluten-free grain similar in appearance to freekeh and offers a protein-rich alternative to carb-heavy grains such as couscous or rice. Its nutty flavor lends itself really well to this powerful dressing. Serve as an accompaniment to Sticky Pomegranate Salmon (*see* page 117).

Buckwheat and Barberry Salad with Spiced Pomegranate Dressing

Serves 6 as a main or 8 as a side

1 cup buckwheat
²⁄₃ cup hot vegetable or chicken stock
⅓ cup unsalted pistachio nuts, coarsely chopped
2 tablespoons dried barberries
1 teaspoon dried mint
1 tablespoon olive oil
2 large handfuls of cilantro, finely chopped

For the pomegranate dressing
1 tablespoon date syrup
1 tablespoon pomegranate molasses
juice of 1 lemon
1 teaspoon ground cumin
1 teaspoon ground sumac
½ teaspoon grated fresh ginger root
½ teaspoon Harissa (*see* page 17)
sea salt and freshly ground black pepper

Place the buckwheat in a sieve and rinse really well under cold running water. Add to a medium saucepan and cover with the hot stock. Bring to a boil, then cover with a lid and let simmer gently for 10 to 12 minutes until the buckwheat is soft but still retains a little bite.

Drain and spread out on a tray or a plate to cool slightly (this prevents it from ending up as one big sticky mass).

Beat the ingredients for the dressing together in a bowl and set aside.

Transfer the buckwheat to a large bowl, then stir in the pistachios, barberries, and mint, add the dressing, and mix it through with a fork. Finish with the olive oil and cilantro, reserving a tablespoon of the latter for garnish. Serve at room temperature, scattered with the reserved cilantro.

Sweets & baking

Some of the best recipes come out of being forced to experiment. Clean out of self-rising and all-purpose flour, I only had wholemeal spelt flour in my kitchen cupboard, which my wheat-free husband uses to make bread. I then decided to try and use up the catering-sized carton of plain yogurt in the fridge and whatever citrus fruit I had. The result was this delicious cake that is lovely and moist and, once topped with yogurt icing and pistachios, becomes wonderfully sticky. I was fortunate enough to inherit Grandma Celia's kugelhopf pan, which has to be at least 60 years old, and while I'm not quite the baker she was, that pan can make anything look impressive.

Yogurt, Pistachio and Orange Kugelhopf

Serves 8

1¼ cups superfine sugar

3 large eggs

grated zest and juice of 2 large oranges

2½ cups wholemeal or white spelt flour, plus extra for dusting

½ cup unsalted pistachios, ground

2 teaspoons baking powder

1 teaspoon ground cinnamon

full-fat plain yogurt, plus 2 tablespoons for the icing

½ cup vegetable oil, plus extra for greasing

For the topping

⅔ cup confectioners' sugar

¼ cup coarsely chopped unsalted pistachio nuts

Preheat the oven to 350°F. Oil and then flour a kugelhopf or bundt pan really thoroughly.

Beat together the sugar and eggs in an electric stand mixer, or in a bowl with an electric hand-held mixer, until light and fluffy; this will take about 10 minutes. Add the orange zest and juice and give the mixture one final mix before folding in the flour, ground pistachios, baking powder, cinnamon, the cup of yogurt, and the oil; don't overmix the batter.

Pour the cake batter into the prepared pan and bake for 40 to 45 minutes, or until a skewer inserted into the center comes out clean. Let the cake cool completely in the pan before turning it out onto a plate.

While the cake is cooling, mix the remaining 2 tablespoons of yogurt and confectioners' sugar together in a bowl until you have a loose paste of pouring consistency.

Once you have unmolded the cooled cake, drizzle the top generously with the icing, allowing it to spill down the sides and form a puddle in the middle and around the outside. Scatter the cake with the chopped pistachios and serve.

You wouldn't necessarily see cheesecake as a spiritual thing, that is, unless you are Jewish. This ubiquitous dessert is the subject of many a Jewish argument regarding its origins, about which there lots of different opinions and very little consensus. My food hero Claudia Roden once said that cheesecake was one of the first foods that Jews assimilated from their Central European neighbors. The famous New York-style baked cheesecake may be popular among many cheesecake fans, but the lesser-known Israeli version is something spectacular.

I make this cheesecake a lot, as it knows no boundaries in terms of the type of occasion it's appropriate for. I make catering-sized pans of it for parties and it never fails to receive a chorus of praise from the lucky recipients. Because it's a no-bake cheesecake, it means there is little that can go wrong. Just ensure that you use good-quality cream cheese and don't try using any other kind of cookies than petite beurre biscuits for the crust—they are the key ingredient. This needs no accompaniment other than some fresh raspberries to cut through the sweetness. It's rich, velvety, and irresistible, so eat with caution.

Israeli White Chocolate Cheesecake

Makes around 12 slices, or 10 if you're greedy

7oz petit beurre biscuits

1 stick unsalted butter, melted

5½oz white chocolate, broken into pieces

2 sticks unsalted butter, softened

½ cup superfine sugar

1 large egg

1 large egg yolk

1 cup good-quality cream cheese (I recommend Philadelphia)

1 cup full-fat crème fraîche

To prepare the crust, add the petite beurre biscuits to a food processor and blitz to crumbs, then mix with the melted butter.

Press two-thirds of the mixture into an 8 × 11-inch baking pan, flattening it out to form an even layer (reserve the remaining one-third for later). Place the crust in the freezer for 15 minutes until it is set.

Meanwhile, prepare the filling. Put the chocolate in a glass bowl and either set over a saucepan of simmering water, ensuring that the base of the bowl doesn't touch the water, or heat in the microwave in 30-second bursts, until melted. Remove the bowl from the pan and let cool slightly.

While the chocolate is melting and cooling, beat the softened butter, sugar, whole egg, and egg yolk together in an electric stand mixer fitted with the paddle attachment until fluffy (or in a bowl with a wooden spoon and develop some muscle at the same time!); this will take around 10 minutes.

Beat the cream cheese and crème fraîche together in a bowl, then stir in the melted chocolate. Add to the butter and sugar mixture, then carefully fold all the ingredients together.

Spread the mixture evenly over the crust and top with the reserved petite beurre biscuit crumbs. Let set in the fridge for a minimum of 3 hours, but 24 hours is preferable.

An overabundance of apples every year from my tree encourages me to devise creative new ways of using them up. These muffins are an occasional weekend treat for the family, but more often I take them as a gift when joining friends for breakfast, brunch, or lunch.

Apple and Cinnamon Muffins

Makes 12 muffins

2 cups all-purpose flour
1 cup superfine sugar
2 teaspoons baking powder
1 tablespoon ground cinnamon
½ teaspoon table salt
1 large eating apple, peeled, cored, and very finely chopped
1 cup buttermilk
½ stick butter, melted
2 eggs

For the streusel topping
½ cup soft dark brown sugar
¼ cup all-purpose flour
½ teaspoon ground cinnamon
1 tablespoon melted butter

Preheat the oven to 350°F and line a 12-hole muffin pan with paper baking cups.

Combine the flour, superfine sugar, baking powder, cinnamon, and salt together in a large bowl, then stir in the chopped apple.

Beat the buttermilk, melted butter, and eggs together, then add to the flour mixture and stir through gently; don't overmix.

Add enough batter to each baking cup to fill them three-quarters full. Mix all the streusel ingredients together in a small bowl with a fork, then sprinkle generously on top of each muffin.

Bake for 18 minutes until the tops are golden brown and a skewer, when inserted, comes out clean. Let cool in the pan for a further 5 minutes.

Tip

Muffins always look extra impressive when baked in brown, tulip-shaped paper baking cups.

Better known as cinnamon balls, these are the ultimate Passover baked treat. I would make them all the time when I was younger; now I delegate the task to my kids. When they make them they get a little over-excited and end up squishing them heavy-handedly rather than gently flattening them. It means I end up with all sorts of shapes and sizes, but they taste just as good. These are really easy to make and are a brilliant way to use up surplus egg whites.

Cinnamon Biscuits

Makes 20 biscuits

2 egg whites
2 cups ground almonds
½ cup superfine sugar
1 tablespoon ground cinnamon, plus 1 teaspoon
3 tablespoons confectioners' sugar

Preheat the oven to 350°F and line 2 cookie sheets with nonstick parchment paper.

Whip the egg whites in a bowl until stiff.

Mix the ground almonds, sugar, and the tablespoon of cinnamon together in a separate bowl, then fold through the egg whites.

Wet your hands, roll the mixture into balls, gently flatten them with the palm of your hand, and place 1 inch apart on the lined cookie sheets. Bake for 18 to 20 minutes until lightly golden.

Mix the confectioners' sugar and remaining teaspoon of cinnamon together on a plate and spread out, then turn the balls in the mixture while they are still warm, getting them really well coated all over. Let cool completely, then turn them again in the spiced sugar and serve.

This is possibly the only recipe in the book that involves anything technical and a few gadgets, as well as arm power, but the end result is worth it. It's a real showstopper of a dessert and the flecks of black halva studded through the white ice cream are a visual delight and a taste sensation. No churning is called for, but you do need to stay close by for some stirring every now and then. Prepare the halva at least 24 to 36 hours ahead of making the ice cream.

Black Halva and White Chocolate Ice Cream

Serves 6

For the black halva
vegetable or other flavorless oil,
for oiling
²/₃ cup liquid honey
¾ cup tahini
3 teaspoons nigella seeds, finely ground
pinch of sea salt

For the ice cream
1¼ cups milk
1 vanilla bean or 1 teaspoon
vanilla bean paste
4 egg yolks
2 tablespoons superfine sugar
7oz white chocolate, finely chopped
1 cup heavy cream

For the halva, start by lining a 6 x 4½ x 3-inch loaf pan (about 3 cups in capacity) with enough oiled plastic wrap to hang over the sides.

Place the honey in a saucepan and heat until it reaches a temperature of 248°F on the sugar thermometer, at which point a drop of honey should form a ball that can be squashed after being dropped into cold water.

Heat the tahini in a separate saucepan until it reaches a temperature of 122°F on the thermometer.

Add the tahini to the honey and beat for about 8 minutes until the mixture has thickened and come together. Add the ground nigella seeds and salt, stir well, and then pour it into the lined pan. Let cool at room temperature before placing in the fridge for 24 to 36 hours.

For the ice cream, heat the milk and vanilla together in a saucepan to just below boiling point. Whisk the egg yolks and sugar together in a bowl, then very slowly pour a little of the hot milk mixture on top while whisking constantly. Continue adding the remainder of the hot milk mixture until it is all incorporated and then return the mixture to the pan and place over medium heat. Cook, stirring constantly, for around 10 minutes until the sauce has thickened into a light custard consistency. Remove and discard the vanilla bean, if using.

Add the white chocolate and stir until it has melted, then cover the surface of the custard with plastic wrap to stop a skin from forming and let cool.

Take the now-set halva and chop into small pieces.

Whip the heavy cream in a bowl until soft peaks form, then fold through the cooled custard. Add the chopped halva pieces, place in a freezerproof container with a lid, cover, and freeze. Stir the ice cream at 30-minute intervals for around 3 hours, then let freeze completely. It's best served within a few days, that is, if it lasts that long!

Tip

You will have more halva than you need for this recipe, so seal and store what's left in an airtight container in the fridge; it will keep for up to 3 weeks.

This cake is so simple, yet so tasty. It came about during an apple season when I was trying to be more imaginative with ways to use our generous crop. The lovely texture of the streusel on top of the soft cinnamon-infused cake is a real delight and even better when served warm with a generous scoop of vanilla ice cream.

Apple Streusel Cake

Serves 8

½ stick unsalted butter, plus extra for greasing

½ cup milk

1 large egg

1½ cups all-purpose flour

½ teaspoon table salt

2 teaspoons baking powder

1 teaspoon ground cinnamon

½ cup superfine sugar

2 apples, peeled, cored, and finely chopped

For the streusel topping

2 tablespoons all-purpose flour

¼ cup soft dark brown sugar

3 tablespoons cold unsalted butter, diced

1 teaspoon ground cinnamon

Preheat the oven to 400°F. Grease and line the bottom of an 8-inch round cake pan with nonstick parchment paper.

Melt the butter in a saucepan, then add the milk and the egg and whisk together to combine.

Sift all the dry ingredients into a bowl, pour the wet mixture on top, and fold to combine, then stir through the chopped apples until they are well incorporated. Pour the cake batter into the prepared pan.

Place all the ingredients for the streusel topping in a small bowl and mix together with a table knife (I find using fingers makes the butter too soft and harder to work with). Spread the streusel evenly over the batter and bake for 30 minutes until a skewer inserted into the center comes out clean, checking every now and then to ensure that the top doesn't get too brown and covering with a sheet of parchment paper if necessary.

Let the cake cool in the baking pan for 10 minutes before removing. Serve warm.

Far less challenging than you might think to make, this renowned loaf holds a very powerful significance in Jewish culture and tradition. Two loaves are made for Friday night in commemoration of the Israelites who were exiled from Egypt and as a reminder that God will provide as long as Jews refrain from working on the Sabbath. Traditionally, a prayer for the challah is spoken before the bread is torn and a piece given to each person around the table. In my house, thick slices of the bread are then cut and dunked into Chicken Soup (*see* page 66), or smothered in Chopped Liver (*see* page 63) and Egg and Onion (*see* page 62). I bake two loaves simply because the kids love it so much, and it makes a lovely French toast for a weekend treat (*see* page 206).

Challah

Makes 2 loaves

4¾ cups (1¼lb) white bread flour, plus extra for dusting

4 egg yolks

⅓ cup vegetable oil, plus extra for oiling

½ cup superfine sugar

1 tablespoon active dry yeast

½ teaspoon table salt

1 cup water

For the glaze

1 egg, beaten

2 tablespoons sesame seeds (optional)

Put all the ingredients for the challah (except the glaze) in a large bowl and bring everything together with your hands until you have formed a dough. Alternatively, you could use the dough setting on your bread machine if you have one.

Turn the dough out onto a floured work surface and knead for 5 minutes until it is smooth and elastic. Place in a large, lightly oiled bowl, cover with a clean dish cloth or plastic wrap, and let stand in a warm place to rise until doubled in size; this should take 1½ hours.

Remove the dough from the bowl and divide into 6 equal portions. Roll 3 of the pieces into long ropes each about 18 inches long and join them together at the top. Then braid the pieces to the end and join again at the bottom. Repeat with the remaining 3 pieces of dough to make a second loaf.

Place the 2 loaves on a cookie sheet lined with nonstick parchment paper, cover, and let rise in a warm, draft-free place for 30 minutes more. Meanwhile, preheat the oven to 340°F.

Brush the challah with the beaten egg to glaze and sprinkle with the sesame seeds, if you like, then bake for 30 to 35 minutes until golden brown and the base of the bread sounds hollow when tapped. Let cool on a wire rack.

Note

Cholla or challah—however you choose to spell it, the "c" is always silent.

It was a very rare occurrence but sometimes my family would find ourselves with leftover challah. Now we always make sure we have extra so that the kids can enjoy challah French toast, a firm favorite at the breakfast table on a Sunday morning.

Challah French Toast with Sour Cherry Jam and Whipped Vanilla Mascarpone

Serves 4

3 eggs

⅓ cup milk

2 tablespoons date syrup

1 teaspoon vanilla extract, plus ½ teaspoon for the cream

4 large, thick slices of Challah (*see page 204*)

1 tablespoon sunflower oil

1 tablespoon butter

⅓ cup mascarpone cheese

⅓ cup heavy cream

2 tablespoons sour cherry jam

1 tablespoon confectioners' sugar, for dusting

Beat the eggs, milk, date syrup, and the 1 teaspoon of vanilla together in a shallow bowl large enough to hold the challah slices in a single layer.

Add the challah slices and let soak for 5 minutes, turning them over a few times.

Heat the oil and the butter in a large skillet until it is sizzling. Fry the challah over medium heat for 2 to 3 minutes on each side until golden.

Meanwhile, beat the mascarpone, cream, and remaining ½ teaspoon of vanilla together in a bowl with an electric mixer until soft peaks form.

Place the challah on a plate and top with some of the sour cherry jam and a generous dollop of the mascarpone cream. Dust with the confectioners' sugar and serve.

I love flourless cakes. They taste light and make me feel slightly virtuous eating them. Dates, nuts, and chocolate are three of my favorite ingredients, so what better idea than to design a cake recipe where they make the perfect match?

Chocolate, Date, and Pistachio Cake

Serves 8

vegetable or other flavorless oil or butter, for oiling/greasing

½ cup superfine sugar

4 eggs, 2 of them separated

¾ cup ground almonds

3 tablespoons unsweetened cocoa powder

⅔ cup finely chopped pitted dates

¾ cup finely chopped unsalted pistachio nuts, plus extra to decorate

7oz dark chocolate, minimum 70% cocoa solids, finely chopped, or chocolate chips

Preheat the oven to 350°F and oil/grease and line a 6 x 4½ x 3-inch loaf pan (about 3 cups in capacity) with nonstick parchment paper.

Beat the sugar, the 2 whole eggs, and 2 egg yolks together in an electric stand mixer fitted with the whisk attachment or in a bowl with an electric hand mixer until pale, thick, and fluffy; this will take around 10 minutes.

Meanwhile, mix the ground almonds, cocoa powder, dates, pistachios, and chocolate together in a large bowl. Fold this almond mixture through the sugar and egg mixture, ensuring that everything is well combined.

Clean out the bowl you used for the almond mixture and add the 2 egg whites. Beat them until they are stiff. Fold gently through the cake batter.

Add the batter to the prepared loaf pan and bake for 40 to 45 minutes or until a skewer inserted into the center of the cake comes out clean.

Let the cake cool in the pan for 10 minutes and then remove and scatter with chopped pistachios. Cut into thick slices to serve.

These truffles came about during *MasterChef* when I needed to find a third date recipe to join my date brûlée and baklava with date syrup. The brief was to make it "thick, brown, and sticky," and I took that brief literally. Given the contraints of time—two hours to make three desserts—I thought these dark, sticky gems would work well. Adding Amaretto elevates the truffles to an indulgent treat.

Date, Pecan and Amaretto Truffles

Makes about 15 truffles

½ cup pitted dates

⅔ cup pecan halves

½ cup unsweetened cocoa powder

2 tablespoons Amaretto

1 tablespoon coconut oil

¼ cup desiccated coconut

Place the dates in a food processor and pulse a few times to break them down. Add the pecans and cocoa powder and blend to combine. Then add the Amaretto and oil and blend again until the mixture comes together.

Scatter the desiccated coconut onto a plate. Take a heaped teaspoonful of the mixture and roll into a ball, then roll the ball in the coconut. Repeat with the remaining mixture.

Set the balls into petit four cups and seal in an airtight container. Store in a cool, dark place until ready to serve. They will keep for up to 2 weeks.

Kosher laws prohibit the mixing of milk and meat, which means that you either have to get creative and think of dairy-free (*pareve*) desserts to serve after a meat meal, or serve a fish or vegetarian main. While it's hard to beat a classic banoffee pie—with a crust of graham cracker crumbs, of course, and not pastry—this stands up really well as a great pareve substitute without suffering any hardship. This is more of an assembly job than any serious cooking, but you do need to start the prep the night before you plan to serve by placing the can of coconut milk in the fridge so that it has a creamy consistency for whipping.

Tahini Banoffee Sundae

Serves 4

1 cup walnut halves

1 tablespoon sesame seeds

½ cup superfine sugar

14oz can coconut milk, chilled overnight in the fridge

2 tablespoons confectioners' sugar

½ teaspoon vanilla extract

¾ cup tahini

¼ cup liquid honey

4 bananas

Preheat the oven to 350°F.

Spread the walnuts and sesame seeds out on a baking pan and roast in the oven for 8 to 10 minutes.

Meanwhile, place the superfine sugar in a dry saucepan over medium heat and wait for it turn a deep amber color—don't stir, otherwise the sugar will crystallize.

When the caramel is ready, add the roasted nuts and seeds and stir quickly to combine, then tip out onto a silicone baking mat or a sheet of foil and set aside until cool enough to handle.

Break the caramel into chunks, add to a food processor, and pulse until you have coarse crumbs; don't overwork the mixture, as you want to retain some texture. Set aside.

Open the can of coconut milk and add only the firm solids from the top of the can to the bowl of an electric stand mixer fitted with the whisk attachment, or a large bowl, along with the confectioners' sugar and vanilla. Whip the ingredients together, with an electric hand mixer if you don't have a stand mixer, until you have a stiff consistency; this will take about 5 minutes.

Whisk the tahini and honey together in a bowl to combine.

To assemble, start by adding some slices of banana to the bottoms of 4 short, straight-sided glasses or glass dessert bowls. Top with a spoonful of the tahini mixture, followed by the coconut mixture, and then the caramel-nut mixture. Repeat the layering—you should get at least 2 layers in each glass—making sure you finish with a very generous sprinkling of the caramel-nut mixture.

Tip

You can make the caramel-nut mixture and tahini and honey paste ahead of time, but the coconut cream will need to be whipped just before serving and the bananas sliced at the last minute to avoid discoloring.

As a woman of little patience, I have never been that enthusiastic about making bread. It's the waiting for it to rise that I find a bit tedious. I do, however, take enormous pleasure in making this sweet Polish bread stuffed full of chocolate and butter, which works so well in this pudding with its double whammy of chocolate. While ready-made chocolate brioche could serve the same purpose, I would advocate trying homemade; the sense of satisfaction alone makes it so worthwhile. This is an ideal make-ahead dessert, as it positively benefits from sitting in the fridge for up to two days before cooking. I've offered quantities to make two loaves at the same time so that you get more for the effort involved—use one for the pudding and freeze the other for later use, if you can resist the temptation to scoff it straight from the oven.

Chocolate Babka Bread and Butter Pudding

Serves 8 to 10

For the bread
¾ cup milk
1 cup superfine sugar, divided
3 teaspoons active dry yeast
3½ cups all-purpose flour, divided, plus extra for dusting
2 large eggs
1 large egg yolk
1 teaspoon almond extract
½ teaspoon table salt
1½ sticks unsalted butter, softened, plus extra for greasing

For the chocolate filling
2 tablespoons unsalted butter, softened
1¼ cups dark chocolate chips
2 tablespoons superfine sugar
1 egg, beaten

For the chocolate custard
6oz dark chocolate, minimum 70% cocoa solids, broken into pieces, or use 1 cup chocolate chips
⅓ cup superfine sugar
1¾ cups heavy cream, plus extra to serve
½ stick unsalted butter
3 large eggs
2 tablespoons cocoa powder

Start by making the bread. Heat the milk in a small saucepan or in the microwave—you want it warm but not hot. Add the milk to the bowl of an electric stand mixer fitted with a paddle attachment with 2 teaspoons of the sugar. Sprinkle with the yeast and let stand for about 5 minutes, or until the mixture is frothy. If it doesn't froth, you need to start the process again, as the bread dough won't rise properly.

Add ¼ cup of the flour to the yeast mixture and mix on medium speed to combine. Add the whole eggs, egg yolk, almond extract, salt, and remaining sugar and continue to beat until everything is incorporated. Reduce the speed to low and gradually add the remaining flour, a tablespoon at a time. Increase the speed again and start adding the butter, a thumb-sized piece at a time, allowing each piece to be fully incorporated before adding the next.

The dough will now be shiny and very sticky—don't be alarmed at this stage, as it will come together nicely! Scrape the sticky mixture into a lightly greased bowl large enough to allow the dough to rise to double the size. Cover with plastic wrap and let stand in a warm place to rise; this can take up to 2 hours.

Line 2 × 2-pound loaf pans (about 8½ x 4½ x 2¼ inches in size) with a double sheet of nonstick parchment paper, one running crosswise and one lengthwise, or use ready-made loaf-pan liners. Halve the risen dough and place one half on a well-floured surface (return the other half to the bowl and re-cover with plastic wrap). Using a floured rolling pin, roll the dough into a rectangle measuring 18 × 10 inches. With a long side nearest to you and leaving a 1-inch border all the way around, spread half the butter for the filling over the dough, then sprinkle half the chocolate chips and sugar evenly over the top. Brush the border with some of the beaten egg and, starting from the long side farthest away from you, roll the dough into a tight log shape. Bring either end of the log together and then pinch them together to ensure that they are well sealed. Carefully twist the ring twice to make a double figure-eight and place in one of the lined loaf pans. Repeat with the remaining half of the dough and filling to make the second loaf.

Cover both loaf pans with oiled plastic wrap and let stand in a warm place to rise until doubled in size; again, this can take up to 2 hours. Meanwhile, preheat the oven to 350°F.

Once risen, brush both the loaves with the remaining beaten egg and bake for around 30 to 40 minutes until golden brown and the base of the bread sounds hollow when tapped. Remove the loaves from the pans and let cool completely on a wire rack.

At this point, you can seal one of the loaves in a double layer of plastic wrap and foil and freeze for later use; it will keep for up to a month.

For the pudding, grease a 2-quart baking dish. Cut the cooled bread into slices, then cut each slice diagonally in half to make triangles. Set aside.

To make the custard, put the chocolate, sugar, cream, and butter in a glass bowl and either set over a saucepan of simmering water, ensuring that the base of the bowl doesn't touch the water, or heat in the microwave in 30-second bursts, until everything has melted together.

In a large, separate bowl, beat the eggs until light and fluffy and then add the melted chocolate mixture along with the cocoa powder. Beat the mixture again, then pour about one-third of the custard into the baking dish. Add the triangles of bread, layering as you go, until the whole dish is covered. Pour the remaining custard evenly over the top, ensuring that all the pieces of bread are coated. Lightly press the top of the bread with a fork so that it is fully immersed in the custard, then cover with plastic wrap and place in the fridge for a minimum of 2 hours, but anything up to 2 days is great.

When you are ready to bake, preheat the oven to 400°F. Bake, uncovered, for 30 minutes until the top is crunchy and golden. Remove from the oven and let sit for approximately 10 minutes before serving with a generous drizzle of heavy cream.

My mother-in-law fondly recalls enjoying this as a hot drink in the markets of Jerusalem on cold winter nights. Getting her thumbs-up for this recipe was very important to me before I could present it to the *MasterChef* judges, and although I knew it would divide the crowd, I was prepared to take the risk to bring something new and different to the table. It's traditionally known as *sahlab*, the name for a flour made from the tubers of an orchid, and depending on which part of the Middle East you are from, it's either enjoyed hot as a winter warmer or cold as a dessert. This is a lovely sweet pudding, fragrant with rosewater and cinnamon, and best enjoyed cold when it's nice and thick with a generous scattering of toasted nuts and coconuts.

Almond and Rosewater Rice Pudding

Serves 6

⅓ cup ground rice

3 tablespoons cornstarch

2½ pints milk, divided

⅓ cup superfine sugar

1 tablespoon rosewater

½ cup ground almonds, divided

½ cup desiccated coconut

2 tablespoons sliced almonds

¼ cup unsalted pistachio nuts

3 tablespoons date syrup

To decorate
ground cinnamon
large handful of edible dried rose petals
(optional)

Mix the ground rice and cornstarch with enough of the milk to make a paste. Place the remaining milk in a saucepan over low heat and bring gently to a boil. Add the sugar and simmer gently for 2 to 3 minutes. Gradually add the ground rice and cornstarch paste, stirring constantly with a wooden spoon to stop it from sticking to the bottom of the pan. Simmer over very low heat for around 10 to 15 minutes, or until the mixture is nice and thick.

Add the rosewater a teaspoonful at a time and check for flavor; it can be overpowering, so add to taste. Stir in half the ground almonds and simmer for another few minutes.

Turn off the heat and let the mixture cool for around 10 minutes.

While the rice pudding is cooling, heat a dry skillet over medium heat, add the coconut, and toast for a few minutes, then set aside. Toast the sliced almonds in the same pan. Cut the pistachios into slivers or lightly crush them, then set aside.

Divide the rice pudding among 6 glass dessert dishes, filling each one around three-quarters full. Drizzle each serving with date syrup and sprinkle with a generous pinch of the toasted coconut, the remaining ground almonds, and the pistachios, then scatter with the toasted sliced almonds, and sprinkle with some cinnamon. Finish by scattering with edible dried rose petals, if you like.

For me, sticky toffee pudding was always the ultimate dessert to choose on a menu. Rich and gooey with melting vanilla ice cream on top, I can fondly recall scraping every last drop of the thick brown sauce from my spoon, always wanting a few bites more. These slightly enhanced, generously-sized individual puddings are a real crowd-pleaser, particularly in the cold winter months when a dessert has to be hot, sticky, and very comforting. Serve with a large scoop of good-quality vanilla ice cream or drizzle with heavy cream.

Cherry Sticky Toffee Puddings with Caramelized Pecans and Tangerine Sauce

Serves 6

2/3 stick unsalted butter, softened, plus extra for greasing
1½ cups dried cherries, divided
2/3 cup boiling water
2 tablespoons Cointreau or other orange-flavored liqueur of your choice
½ teaspoon baking soda
¾ cup superfine sugar
2 eggs, beaten
1½ cups self-rising flour sifted with
1½ teaspoons baking powder

For the caramelized pecans
½ stick butter
1 cup pecan halves
¼ cup soft dark brown sugar

For the sauce
1 cup light brown sugar
1 stick unsalted butter
1/3 cup heavy cream
¼ cup pecan halves, chopped
juice of 1 tangerine

Preheat the oven to 350°F.

Lightly grease 6 individual metal pudding bowls or ramekins, then line the bottom of each with a disk of nonstick parchment paper.

Put 1¼ cups of the dried cherries into a bowl and add the measured boiling water. Stir in the liqueur and baking soda, then let sit for an hour.

Cream the butter and superfine sugar together in a large bowl until pale and fluffy, then slowly beat in the eggs a little at a time. Add the cherry mixture, then the flour, and fold in with a large metal spoon.

Divide the batter equally among the prepared bowls or ramekins, place on a baking pan, and bake for around 25 minutes until well risen and firm.

Let the puddings cool in the bowls or dishes while you prepare the nuts and the sauce.

For the caramelized pecans, melt the butter in a saucepan over medium heat, then add the pecans and stir well to coat. Add the brown sugar and stir until the nuts have caramelized. Pour out onto a sheet of nonstick parchment paper and let cool and harden.

To make the sauce, put the light brown sugar, butter, cream, pecans, and remaining cherries in a saucepan. Heat gently until the sugar has dissolved, then stir in the tangerine juice.

Turn each pudding out onto a plate and top with the sauce and the caramelized pecans.

Variation

You can replace the cherries with any other dried fruit of your choice.

This is one of my favorite showstopping desserts. The crunchiness of the pastry crust against the light frangipane filling along with the soft fruit is a winning combination, and the colors make this as pleasing on the eye as it is on the palate. Ripe apricots are my first choice of stone fruit here, but white peaches also work really well when in season. *Mahleb* (also known as *mahlepi*, among other variants) powder is produced by grinding the seed kernels from the stones of the St. Lucie cherry, and has a bitter almond-cherry flavor.

Apricot and Orange Blossom Frangipane with Pistachios

Serves 8 to 10

For the pastry
1½ cups all-purpose flour, plus extra for dusting
1 teaspoon mahleb (mahlepi) powder
pinch of table salt
1½ sticks cold unsalted butter, cubed
¼ cup confectioners' sugar
2 egg yolks

For the frangipane
1½ sticks unsalted butter, softened, plus extra for greasing
1 cup superfine sugar
1 cup whole blanched almonds
2 eggs
1 tablespoon orange blossom water
6 ripe apricots, halved and stoned
2 tablespoons chopped unsalted pistachio nuts

Place the flour, mahleb powder, salt, and butter in a food processor and pulse to combine. Add the confectioners' sugar and egg yolks and pulse until the mixture starts to come together into a dough.

Turn out onto a lightly floured work surface and gather into a ball. Then seal in plastic wrap and refrigerate for an hour.

Grease a 9-inch fluted tart pan with a removable bottom. Grate the pastry dough coarsely into the tart pan, making sure that the bottom and sides are evenly covered and there are no gaps. Return to the fridge for a further 30 minutes. Meanwhile, preheat the oven to 400°F.

Line the pastry crust with a sheet of nonstick parchment paper and fill with ceramic baking beans or rice, then bake blind for 15 minutes. Carefully remove the paper with the beans or rice (some of the pastry may separate, so gently press back together with the back of a spoon) and bake, uncovered, for a further 10 minutes until lightly golden. Let the crust cool completely while you make the filling. Reduce the oven temperature to 340°F.

Cream the softened butter and sugar together in an electric stand mixer fitted with the paddle attachment or in a bowl with a wooden spoon until pale and light.

Add the almonds to a food processor and pulse to a coarse rubble; you don't want powder, so be careful not to overwork them. Beat the almonds into the butter and sugar, then beat in the eggs, one at a time, and finally add the orange blossom water, mixing until everything is combined.

Spoon the frangipane mixture into the crust and top with the apricot halves, cut-side up. Bake for 50 minutes. Remove from the oven and scatter with the chopped pistachios, then bake for a further 20 minutes.

Let the tart cool completely in the pan before removing and slicing.

Baklava is the ultimate Middle Eastern treat with all the key attributes: sweetness, stickiness, and nuttiness. My version of these little delicacies, contains a few more spices (of course) and a drizzle of chocolate at the end (why not?) just to give it that extra hit of sugar.

Baklava with Chocolate Drizzle

Makes 24 generous pieces

For the baklava
2 cups pecan halves
²/₃ cup unsalted pistachio nuts, plus extra to decorate
1 cup whole unblanched almonds
1 stick unsalted butter
1 teaspoon vanilla bean paste
1/3 cup soft dark brown sugar
1/2 teaspoon ground cardamom
1 teaspoon ground mixed spice
1 teaspoon ground cinnamon
pinch of freshly grated nutmeg
2 x 9½oz packs of filo pastry sheets
1/2 cup dark chocolate chips, melted, to decorate

For the syrup
3/4 cup water
1/2 cup granulated sugar
2 tablespoons date syrup
1 teaspoon vanilla bean paste
1 cinnamon stick

Preheat the oven to 375°F.

Spread all the nuts evenly out on a 12 x 8-inch baking pan and toast in the oven for 10 minutes.

Meanwhile, melt the butter in a small saucepan over low heat.

When the nuts are ready, tip into a food processor and pulse until finely chopped but still with some coarse pieces. Alternatively, chop the nuts by hand. Add the vanilla bean paste and give one final stir. Transfer the nut mixture to a bowl, add the sugar and spices, and stir to combine.

Grease the 12 × 8-inch baking pan with some of the melted butter and cut the filo sheets to fit. The best way to avoid pastry wastage is to place your pan vertically on one half of the pastry sheet, and if it is approximately half, you can cut straight down the middle to give you double the sheets.

Add the first sheet of pastry to the pan and liberally brush it with the melted butter using a pastry brush, then repeat 6 times. Scatter a generous layer of nuts on top, then splash some melted butter over the nuts with the brush to help the first sheet of pastry stick to the nuts. Repeat the layering using another 4 filo sheets, spreading each sheet with more melted butter each time. Add another layer of nuts before finishing with the final 6 sheets, then give the top sheet a good coating of melted butter.

Place the pan in the fridge for 30 minutes, or up to 24 hours if making ahead.

Put all the ingredients for the syrup in a saucepan over medium heat, stir, and bring to a rolling boil, then reduce the heat and simmer for 10 minutes, stirring often, until thickened.

When ready to bake, preheat the oven to 350°F.

Remove the baklava from the fridge. Set the pan horizontally and cut across the baklava from left to right in a series of diagonal lines spaced about 1¼ inches apart, then repeat in the other direction. Bake for 20 to 25 minutes, rotating the pan halfway through to ensure that the top browns evenly.

Remove the baklava from the oven and immediately pour the syrup evenly over the top, discarding the cinnamon stick, making sure that you coat all the pieces evenly. If you have the time (and the willpower), let the baklava sit and cool completely so that the syrup can fully soak in.

Drizzle with the melted chocolate and scatter with chopped pistachios.

Natalie Allen, the lovely owner of the Sweet Things bakery in Primrose Hill and Notting Hill Gate in London, was kind enough to share this delicious recipe with me. Make sure you use really good-quality dark chocolate, as you need that lovely rich, slightly bitter flavor to counteract the sweetness.

Chocolate Fondant Cake

Serves 8 to 10

unsweetened cocoa powder, for dusting

7oz good-quality dark chocolate, minimum 70% cocoa solids, broken into pieces

1¾ sticks butter, plus extra for greasing (or use vegetable oil)

¾ cup superfine sugar

5 eggs

1 tablespoon all-purpose flour (gluten-free flour is fine)

To serve
vanilla ice cream
raspberries

Preheat the oven to 375°F.

Grease an 8-inch springform cake pan with butter or oil and dust with unsweetened cocoa powder; you won't need to line the pan if you do this thoroughly enough.

Put the chocolate and butter together in a glass bowl and either set over a saucepan of simmering water, ensuring that the base of the bowl doesn't touch the water, or heat in the microwave in 30-second bursts, until melted.

Stir in the sugar, then add the eggs, one at a time, beating in each one with a wooden spoon before adding the next. Add the flour and mix well, then transfer to the prepared pan.

Bake for 20 to 25 minutes; the cake should still tremble in the middle. Let cool completely in the pan, then serve at room temperature, or serve chilled with some vanilla ice cream and raspberries.

My mom's rum chocolate mousse was legendary. I think this recipe was adapted from an Evelyn Rose cookbook that she loved, but whether the famous Jewish cook herself used quite as much rum as Mom is something we will never know. The absence of dairy (if using kosher chocolate) makes it a great pareve dessert. Use dark chocolate only for a kosher option; it will just be a little richer.

Rum Chocolate Mousse

Serves 8

7oz dark chocolate, minimum 70% cocoa solids, broken into pieces

5½oz milk chocolate, broken into pieces (*see above*)

2 tablespoons dark rum

8 eggs, separated

Put the chocolate with the rum in a glass bowl and either set over a saucepan of simmering water, ensuring that the base of the bowl doesn't touch the water, or heat in the microwave in 30-second bursts, until melted. Let the melted chocolate mixture cool a little, then gradually stir in the egg yolks.

Beat the egg whites in a separate large bowl until stiff, then gently fold through the chocolate mixture.

Pour the mousse into a bowl of your choice, cover with plastic wrap, and place in the fridge to set for a minimum of 6 hours.

The recipe for this cake came from the lovely students at Les Roches Royal Academy of Culinary Arts in Jordan where I was fortunate enough to enjoy a meal cooked by them. I love all things simple when they taste this good. There is no need to use fancy olive oil, but the flavor is more robust if you use a stronger-flavored one like extra virgin. Just a few simple raspberries or strawberries on top are all it needs to shine.

Olive Oil Cake

Serves 10 to 12

1 cup superfine sugar, divided
2 large egg yolks
2 tablespoons fresh lemon juice
grated zest of ½ lemon
1 cup all-purpose flour
⅔ cup olive oil, plus extra for oiling
3 egg whites
pinch of table salt
raspberries and strawberries, to serve

Preheat the oven to 350°F. Oil and line the bottom of a 9-inch cake pan with a removable bottom.

Place three-quarters of the sugar, the egg yolks, and the lemon juice and zest into the bowl of an electric stand mixer fitted with a paddle attachment and beat together for 5 minutes, scraping down the sides once or twice, or use a bowl and wooden spoon if making by hand. Slowly add the flour and mix for 2 minutes, then drizzle in the olive oil and continue to beat until it is well combined and glossy. Transfer the batter to another bowl and clean out the mixing bowl. Replace the paddle attachment with the beaters, or use an electric hand mixer and a clean bowl.

Add the egg whites and salt to the mixing bowl and beat until stiff. Gradually add the remaining sugar and continue to beat until the mixture forms stiff peaks.

Fold the egg white mixture into the cake batter in 3 stages until combined. Add to the prepared pan and bake for 25 to 30 minutes or until a skewer inserted into the center of the cake comes out clean. Set aside to cool completely in the pan. Don't be alarmed if the cake starts to crack as it cools; it's all part of the charm.

Scatter with raspberries and strawberries before serving.

Matzo is traditionally eaten over Passover when the consumption of leavened products containing the five forbidden grains—wheat, barley, oats, rye, and spelt, known as *chametz*—is prohibited. Kitchen cupboards become stuffed full of these delicious crackers and the quest begins to try and be as creative as possible with them for the eight days of the "feast without the yeast." We tend to eat matzo all year round, simply because this eggy breakfast delicacy with a generous sprinkle of cinnamon sugar is the kids' absolute favorite weekend breakfast, and even better that it's Daddy wearing the apron for a change.

Carl's Matzo Brei

Serves 2

3 large matzo squares
¾ cup boiling water
2 eggs, beaten
¼ teaspoon table salt
1 tablespoon unsalted butter
½ teaspoon ground cinnamon
3 teaspoons granulated sugar

Break the matzo sheets into approximately 1-inch pieces or, better still, get the kids to do it. Add to a bowl and add the measured boiling water. Give it a stir, then cover with a plate or plastic wrap, and let stand for 5 minutes until the matzo pieces have softened.

Add the eggs and salt and mix until everything is combined.

Melt the butter in a skillet over medium heat, add the matzo mixture, and flatten down with a spatula to make a large pancake. Cook for 3 minutes, then check if the underside is golden and use the spatula to cut the pancake into quarters. Turn the pieces over and cook for a further 3 to 4 minutes until golden brown. Transfer the matzo brei to a plate.

Mix the cinnamon and sugar together, then sprinkle over the top of the matzo brei. Eat immediately.

Arabic desserts are always very sweet, heavily laden as they are with sugar syrup, and this cake is no exception. It is, however, so moist and tasty that you can almost momentarily forget about the calorie content. I slightly adapted this recipe from the wonderful Abbey Road restaurant, run by Chef Hani, in Madaba, Jordan.

Semolina and Coconut "Harese" Cake

Serves around 15

2 cup fine semolina
2¾ cups desiccated coconut
1 cup superfine sugar
1 heaped teaspoon baking powder
2 cups full-fat plain yogurt
¾ cup corn oil
½ stick unsalted butter, melted
2 tablespoons light tahini

For the sugar syrup
1½ cups superfine sugar
¾ cup water

Preheat the oven to 425°F.

First make the sugar syrup. Put the sugar and measured water into a saucepan, bring to a boil, and cook for 10 minutes over medium heat until the sugar has dissolved and the mixture has slightly thickened. Let cool while you make the cake.

Mix all the ingredients except the tahini together in a large bowl, stirring well to make sure that everything is properly combined.

Using a pastry brush, spread the tahini over the bottom of a 12 × 9½-inch baking pan, add the cake batter, and spread it out evenly.

Bake for 18 minutes until the top is springy and lightly golden. Let the cake cool in the pan for 10 minutes, then pour the sugar syrup evenly over the top. Let the cake cool completely before cutting into generous squares.

This beloved classic Jewish pudding is a cross between a crème brûlée and a cheesecake in taste and consistency. A real departure from the stodgy and rather bland noodle kugel I grew up eating, I apologize in advance to those I offend with its much-needed makeover.

Sweet Noodle Kugel

Serves 10 to 12

1 Earl Grey tea bag
¾ cup boiling water
1¼ cups golden raisins
10½oz dried egg noodles (I like Manischewitz from the kosher section)
½ stick butter, plus extra for greasing
4 eggs
1 cup ricotta cheese
1²⁄₃ cups full-fat cream cheese
¾ cup superfine sugar
2 tablespoons ground cinnamon
grated zest of 1 orange
2 teaspoons orange blossom water

For the brûlée topping
⅓ cup light brown raw cane sugar
1 tablespoon sesame seeds

Preheat the oven to 400°F and lightly grease a 12 × 9½-inch baking dish.

Place the tea bag in a bowl, add the measured boiling water, and let brew for 2 to 3 minutes, then add the golden raisins. Cover and let stand for as long as possible, up to 24 hours, but ideally at least an hour.

Cook the noodles in a saucepan of salted boiling water following the package directions, until tender. Drain, add the butter, and fork through.

Beat the eggs and cheeses together in a bowl with a wooden spoon, or use an electric stand mixer fitted with the paddle attachment, until smooth. Discard the tea bag and add the golden raisins along with their soaking liquid to the cheese mixture. Then add the superfine sugar, cinnamon, orange zest, and orange blossom water. Add the noodles and give the mixture a good stir to combine. Transfer to the greased dish and bake for 30 minutes until set.

For the brûlée topping, preheat the broiler to its highest setting. Mix the light brown raw cane sugar with the sesame seeds and scatter evenly over the cooked kugel. Broil the kugel until the sugar is golden and bubbling. This is best eaten hot, but it's also delicious cold.

My mother-in-law fondly recalls her mother making ma'amoul cookies when she was a little girl, the filling of lightly spiced dates oozing out of the centers of their very light, crumbly shells. Having enjoyed these cookies myself across the Middle East, I wanted to do justice to my mother-in-law's memory. These are traditionally made using a beautiful wooden ma'amoul mold (available on online for less than $15). While it's not essential to the taste, it is to their delightful appearance, so I would strongly urge you to buy one.

Spiced Date "Ma'amoul" Cookies

Makes 45 cookies

¼ teaspoon active dry yeast

3 tablespoons tepid water

2 sticks unsalted butter, at room temperature

3 tablespoons vegetable oil, plus extra for oiling the mold if using

⅔ cup confectioners' sugar, plus extra for dusting

½ teaspoon orange blossom water

1 teaspoon vanilla extract

pinch of table salt

1 heaped teaspoon mahleb (mahlepi) powder

4 cups all-purpose flour, sifted

For the date filling

1 cup pitted Medjool dates

½ teaspoon vegetable oil

1 teaspoon ground cinnamon

½ teaspoon ground allspice

½ teaspoon ground nutmeg

¼ teaspoon ground ginger

Preheat the oven to 350°F. Line 2 large cookie sheets with nonstick parchment paper.

Add the yeast to a bowl, mix in the tepid water, and let sit for 5 minutes.

Beat the butter and oil together in an electric stand mixer fitted with the paddle attachment for about 3 minutes until well combined, or use a large bowl and a wooden spoon if making by hand. Add the confectioners' sugar and continue to beat until it is incorporated, then add the yeast mixture, orange blossom water, and vanilla extract and continue to beat on a slow speed. With the machine running, add the salt and mahleb powder, then add the flour, a little at a time, until it is combined. Continue to beat for another minute, then transfer the dough to a bowl. Let it rest for 15 minutes while you make the date filling.

Coarsely chop the dates, add to a food processor with the oil, and blend until you have a thick paste, or finely chop if you don't have a food processor. Add the spices and mix them in well.

Take a walnut-sized amount of the dough, roll it into a ball, and then form it into a bowl by turning it around and using your thumb and forefinger to make a hole wide enough to add the filling. Place a teaspoonful of the filling in the hole, then bring the top of the dough over the filling to cover it and reshape into a ball. Lightly oil your mold, if using, and add the ball, pressing it into the shape. To remove the dough from the mold, hold the handle, turn it over, and tap it onto a wooden board. Continue with the remaining dough, placing the cookies on the lined sheets about ½ inch apart.

If you don't have a mold, proceed as above by rolling the dough into balls, filling, and sealing, but press down on the top of the balls with the tines of a fork to make a pretty pattern.

Bake the cookies for 15 to 18 minutes, rotating the cookie sheets halfway through if necessary, until very pale gold in color; be careful not to overcook.

Let the cookies cool on the cookie sheets for 5 minutes before transferring them to a wire rack. Dust liberally with confectioners' sugar to finish.

This tart celebrates the combination of orange and chocolate beautifully. Rich and indulgent, it makes a killer dinner party dessert for which your guests, no matter how full they may be, will always find room.

Dark Chocolate and Orange Tart

Serves 8 to 10

For the crust
3 cups all-purpose flour, plus extra for dusting
2½ cups confectioners' sugar
¼ cup unsweetened cocoa powder
1¾ sticks cold unsalted butter, cubed, plus extra for greasing
grated zest of 1 orange
1 egg
pinch of table salt

For the filling
1¼ cups heavy whipping cream
8½oz dark chocolate, minimum 70% cocoa solids, finely chopped
2 tablespoons Cointreau or other orange-flavored liqueur of your choice
grated zest of ½ orange

To decorate
grated zest of ½ orange
unsweetened cocoa powder

If you have a food processor, add all the ingredients for the crust to it and pulse until the mixture just comes together in a ball. If making by hand, sift the flour, confectioners' sugar, and cocoa powder together into a bowl, and then, using your fingertips, gently work the butter into the flour mixture until it resembles bread crumbs. Stir in the orange zest, then finally add the egg, beaten, and salt and gently work everything together until you have a ball of dough.

Dust the ball of dough with a little flour, then gently press on it to flatten it into a disk. Seal in plastic wrap and let rest in the fridge for 30 minutes.

Preheat the oven to 400°F and lightly grease a 9-inch tart pan.

Roll the dough out between 2 sheets of nonstick parchment paper or plastic wrap, rotating the pastry after each time you roll it, until it is about ¼ inch thick. Remove the top sheet of paper or plastic wrap and carefully roll the pastry around your rolling pin, then unroll over your tart pan. Gently press the dough into the sides of the pan and remove the top layer of paper or plastic wrap. Trim off any excess dough with a knife, or roll your rolling pin over the top, then prick the bottom all over with a fork and return to the fridge for a further 30 minutes.

Take a sheet of nonstick parchment paper, crunch it into a ball, and then unwrap it and use it to line your tart crust. Fill the crust with ceramic baking beans or rice and bake blind for 15 minutes. Carefully remove the paper with the beans or rice and bake, uncovered, for a further 6 to 8 minutes until golden. Let the tart crust cool completely.

For the filling, bring the cream to a simmer in a saucepan. Remove from the heat, add the chocolate, and stir into the cream to melt, then add the liqueur and orange zest and continue stirring until the mixture is smooth.

Pour the chocolate mixture into the cooled tart crust, and then let stand in the fridge to set for a minimum of 3 hours, covered loosely with foil, but ensuring that the foil doesn't touch the top of the tart. Decorate with grated orange zest and a dusting of unsweetened cocoa powder.

Tip
This tart benefits from being served with something a little sharp to offset the richness, so some berries or unsweetened crème fraîche would work well.

My husband's late grandmother Celia, better known to my kids as Ggma, fled from Vienna in 1938, taking her deep-rooted Austrian values and cherished family recipes with her. Her famous apple strudel is her greatest legacy. I never managed to do it justice when I tried to reconstruct it, so I've replaced the fiddly filo with a light pastry. If you are using a tart variety of apple like Rome Beauty, you will need to add sugar to the filling, but if you have opted for a dessert apple such as Granny Smith, you can leave sugar out of the filling altogether.

I think Ggma would like my version, but I can still imagine her telling me off in her thick German accent for changing hers.

Viennese Apple Turnover

Serves 8

beaten egg white, to glaze

2 tablespoons sliced almonds, for scattering

heavy cream, vanilla ice cream, or custard to serve (optional)

For the dough

5 cups (1 ¼ lb) all-purpose flour, plus extra for dusting

3 ½ sticks cold unsalted butter, cubed

1 ²⁄₃ cups confectioners' sugar, plus 2 tablespoons for dusting

5 large egg yolks, beaten

For the filling

3 ¼ lb cooking apples, such as Rome Beauty, or dessert apples, such as Granny Smith, peeled, cored, and chopped into ¾-inch pieces

¹⁄₃ cup raisins

2 tablespoons ground cinnamon, plus 1 teaspoon for dusting

1 teaspoon ground mixed spice

¼ cup superfine sugar (or more or less depending on the type of apple used)

If you have a food processor, add all the dough ingredients to it and pulse until the mixture just comes together in a ball. If making by hand, add the flour to a bowl, and then, using your fingertips, gently work the butter into the flour until the mixture resembles bread crumbs. Mix in the sugar, then add the egg yolks and work everything together until you have a ball of dough. Seal in plastic wrap and let chill in the fridge for 30 minutes.

Preheat the oven to 400°F.

Divide the dough into a 60:40 ratio, as you want a bit more pastry for the top, then rewrap the larger piece and return to the fridge. Using a rolling pin lightly dusted with flour, roll the smaller piece into a large rectangle about ¾ inch thick on a sheet of nonstick parchment paper; don't worry about making it too uniform, as you will be shaping it later. Transfer to a baking pan and bake, uncovered, for 5 minutes. Remove from the oven and let cool.

For the filling, mix the apples, raisins, and spices together in a bowl, then sprinkle with the sugar. Pile the filling on top of the dough, leaving a ½-inch border around the edge. Roll out the remaining dough on a lightly floured work surface so that it is large enough to cover the filling. Brush the egg white around the border of the bottom layer of dough and lay the larger sheet over the top, making sure that the apple filling is well covered and that the 2 pieces of pastry join. Cut around the edges with a sharp knife to make a neat rectangle and press down with a fork to make a pretty pattern and help ensure that none of the juice from the filling escapes. Using a sharp knife, cut 2 or 3 holes in the top to allow the steam to escape. Glaze the top with beaten egg white and scatter with the sliced almonds. If you have time, place the baking pan in the fridge for 30 minutes.

Bake the turnover for 45 minutes to 1 hour until the top is golden brown. Let cool slightly before mixing the 2 tablespoons confectioners' sugar and cinnamon together and dusting them liberally over the top.

Slice and serve with heavy cream, vanilla ice cream, or custard, if liked.

Index

Acknowledgments

There are a few people I would like to thank for their support, encouragement, and belief in me.

First, my incredible husband and girls, the driving force behind everything I do. Even though I made you all eat a lot, pretty much every day for six months, you always appreciated it (even when some experiments went horribly wrong) and praised me (knowing that criticizing wasn't an option). Carl, you are my rock, and although I may not tell you enough, I couldn't do what I do without you.

To my agent Heather Holden-Brown at HHB Agency who totally got me at our first meeting ever. She said there was a book in me and here I am. I would also like to thank Alison Starling and her amazing team at Octopus for their support, guidance, and more importantly, for giving me this opportunity. Juliette Norsworthy and Leanne Bryan, you were both so lovely to work with. Rosie Reynolds, Clare Winfield and Linda Berlin; you are geniuses with your styling and photography.

To my mom Hilary and sisters Debbie and Samantha for their support and encouragement. My childhood memories of food and mealtimes are always remembered fondly, even when they included tears and tantrums in restaurants for there not being enough food! To my in-laws, particularly Judith and her siblings for their family recipes, and to all extended family members who helped out in many other ways; Ros and Doug, you know who you are!

To my *MasterChef* family, who nurtured me and calmed my nerves through the most stressful experience I have ever known.

To the Jordan Tourist Board and Tara Gandhi at Brighter PR who helped me put together such an incredible experience in my quest to feed my obsession with Middle Eastern food. And now for all the people on the ground who welcomed me into their beautiful country, homes, kitchens, and restaurants. Thank you to Hashem Restaurant, Habibah Sweets, and the RACA (Royal Academy of Culinary Arts) in Amman, Um Amer, Um Hamza, Captain's Desert Camp in Wadi Rum, chef Mohammed Asmar at the Mövenpick Tala Bay in Aqaba, Al Qantarah Restaurant in Petra, and last (but not least) Issam Hirzallah and Haneen Karadsheh for looking after us so well and being such lovely company; your passion and love of your beautiful country knows no limits.

To Helen Graham for your recipe contributions. You are a wonderful, talented chef with killer recipe ideas and a bright future ahead of you, and I loved our experimental foodie sessions in my kitchen.

Thank you also to a very talented lady I met over Instagram, @mandyliciouschallah, for her foolproof challah recipe.

To all my recipe testers: Debbie, Laura, Jo, Julien, and Emma.

To Staub and Zwilling, my culinary partners, for their *crème de la crème* of cookware and knives; cooking is a lot more pleasurable when you have top-notch equipment. To Beloved Dates for the endless supply of your Date Nectar date syrup (I got through bucketloads), Providence Deli, Al Arz Tahini (it's seriously the best I have ever tasted), the incredible shop Pulia in London's Borough Market (Georges, you are a star), Mark at South West Garlic Farm for your supply of black garlic, and to Walter Purkis and Sons, my local fishdealers— how lucky I am to have you around the corner.

I also want to thank my late father Bernie. I didn't tell him enough how special and incredibly influential he was in my life. It's only now that I am married with kids of my own that I can see just how exceptional a father he was. I know how proud he would have been of this book.

Author biography

Emma Spitzer was born and raised in Brighton, southern England, to Jewish parents of Polish and Russian descent.

Her love of cooking started at a very early age. Emma shadowed her mother in the kitchen as she regularly cooked traditional Ashkenazi Jewish dishes passed down from her Polish parents. Emma now loves to draw influences from her travels through the Middle East, her cultural heritage, and her mother-in-law's North African roots. She creates food with lots of passion and lots of spice. Her style is big, bold flavors with many different ingredients coming together on one plate.

Emma's ambition started at an early age; at 28 she set up a travel business selling luxury spa vacations across the world. In 2007 the company launched its award-winning second brand, Tots Too, which offers luxury family vacations worldwide. Following her success on reaching the final of BBC 1's *MasterChef*, Emma has been in high demand. She has been teaching cooking classes and demonstrating at food festivals, running sell-out supper clubs, and catering for private dining events. She lives in north London with her husband, four young daughters, and their cat.